DANISH BALLADS AND FOLK SONGS

DANISH BALLADS

Selected and Edited by ERIK DAL

For what can give a more honest or decent pastime
than such fine ballads
which are so cleverly put together, and contain
so rare fantastic pieces; when read,
they force a man's thought away from
any unease and melancholy.

Woodcuts by MARCEL RASMUSSEN

THE AMERICAN-SCANDINAVIAN FOUNDATION

AND FOLK SONGS

Translated by HENRY MEYER

Certainly I must confesse my own barbarousnes,
I never heard the olde song of Percy and
Duglas, that I found not my heart mooved
more then with a Trumpet.
Above: Sir *Philip Sidney* 1595
Left: *A. S. Vedel* 1591

Copenhagen and New York

ROSENKILDE AND BAGGER · MCMLXVII

 The title of the original edition was: *Danske Viser: Gamle folkeviser. Skæmt. Efterklang*. Rosenkilde and Bagger, Copenhagen 1962. The woodcuts are printed with the original blocks. Book design by Erik Dal. Printed in Denmark by Pedersen & Lefevre.

There was Ebbe Skammelsen, he rode a furious race. (See page 116).

This book is a translation of my *Danske Viser: Gamle Folkeviser, Skæmt, Efterklang* (Copenhagen 1962). There are but minor changes from the original: The introduction has been slightly expanded and revised. The notes have been extended, where consideration for non-Danish readers so requires, and abbreviated where explanation of single words and phrases had become unnecessary. The Danish Number 50 has been replaced by *Lie and Truth,* and Nos. 51 and 52 have changed places, while better sources have been used for Nos. 72 and 73. These changes are exceptions from the rule that the texts of the original and the present edition follow each other page by page so that the Danish and English versions may be easily compared.

Anthologies of Danish ballads for the general public have been published both before and after the initial publication of the scholarly ballad edition *Danmarks gamle Folkeviser* in 1853. Such anthologies were produced by Svend Grundtvig (1867 and 1882), Axel Olrik (*Danske Folkeviser i Udvalg,* 1899–1909), H. Grüner-Nielsen (1925–1927), Ernst von der Recke (1927–29), and Ernst Frandsen (1937 and 1945). I now add myself to their number.

However, also the practice of translating Danish ballads into English is old. Robert Jamieson, George Borrow, "An Amateur" (1858), Robert Buchanan, Alexander Prior, and Alexander Gray in our own day, are to be regarded with gratitude, for they made such selections and translations over the last century and a half. E. M. Smith-Dampier ended her contributions to Scandinavian ballad poetry with a full translation of Olrik's valuable and popular anthology: *A Book of Danish Ballads,* selected and with an introduction by Axel Olrik (Princeton University Press and The American-Scandinavian Foundation, 1939). I am grateful that cooperation was possible between Rosenkilde and Bagger, my Danish publisher, and The American-Scandinavian Foundation, which was represented, in the various negotiations, by Mr. Erik J. Friis.

This present anthology is only partly a collection of ballads. Numbers 38–73 and parts of the Addendum are not ballads, but selections from the best of other old popular genres: humorous ditties, epic songs younger than the ballads, and lyrics. Some are as late as the sensation-seeking broadside prints of the eighteenth century. These additional elements of Danish song tradition are less well known in Denmark than the ballads of medieval origin, because very few examples made their way into the anthologies; and it is hoped that they will enrich the reader's understanding of Danish folk poetry. – The basis of selection in this volume will not be discussed here: There is space for only one out of fifteen relevant song types. An effort has been made to keep the question of quality uppermost in a welter of conflicting claims.

The Danish edition reproduces every item in accordance with the published text of the appropriate scholarly publication or the original source. All the old words and most of the word forms have been kept, but spelling has been updated. The translator has been loyal to this conservative principle. Thus, what is here offered the reader is almost literal translations of unrevised texts, in each case one single version chosen from a varying number of variant versions. The few places where it has been found necessary to interpolate lines or stanzas from other texts or by reconstruction are mentioned in the notes, and normally square brackets have been used.

The variegated character of the pieces and the now and then somewhat unusual choice among versions of a given ballad have greatly increased the translator's difficulties. Any translation, not least a translation of old poetry, may produce disagreement over style. Mr. Henry Meyer maintains the viewpoint – and I am in perfect agreement with him – that the ballad idiom as refined by poets of the nineteenth century tends to sacrifice the original flavor of the ballads handed down by tradition and that it is advisable to dispense with current artistic niceties and stick to the literal facts when original versions of folk ballads are being translated. The medieval-ballad milieu, of course, was admittedly "aristocratic". But the rather consistent style of past centuries lost uniformity down the years, and the translator should not be too insistent upon unifying the style again. Thus, colloquial language, ranging from the slang of the time to more refined expression, is not only the proper language in the proper setting, but also the proper language for the translator.

By the same token, Mr. Henry Meyer has followed the old practice of liberal use of personal pronouns and inverted constructions: these were accepted poetic devices for British and Scandinavian ballad makers and folk singers, and the translators should be allowed to use them freely. – I want to express my sincere gratitude to Henry Meyer for his enthusiastic cooperation.

I must acknowledge here, as in the Danish edition, my debt to my predecessors, especially to the archivist Mr. H. Grüner-Nielsen (d. 1953); to the archivist of the Danish Folklore Archives, Mr. Iørn Piø, with whom I published the latter half-volume of *Danmarks gamle Folkeviser X* and who has provided helpful advice; to other good helpers on both sides of the Atlantic Ocean; to Professor Carl Roos (d. 1962) whose typographic ideas and arrangements have put their impress on my layout of the book. I also want to remember my friend Marcel Rasmussen, the graphic artist, who died in 1964.

The Royal Library, Copenhagen, December 20, 1966.

Erik Dal

CONTENTS

III LATER SONGS

IV ADDENDUM

V NOTES AND INDICES

INTRODUCTION

THE TRADITION. "The sky is full of violins!" With these winged words the Danish literary savant Ernst Frandsen characterized the playing, singing, and dancing Europe of the Middle Ages. The Danish ballad should, of course, be seen both in historical and in musical perspective. We stand with empty hands far too often, however, when we look for solid facts about medieval ballads. For the people of the Middle Ages played, sang, and danced, but did not write, not very much, at least, about the worldly things with which we have to do here. We are lucky whenever we are permitted to rejoice over some living treasure of folk poetry handed down to us somehow, though very little is known about the antiquity of the genres, their diffusion, their original forms, and their music.

• One of the appendixes of this volume, the index of sources, tells the thoughtful reader more than such matter usually does. Note that the brief list is arranged systematically and at the same time is almost chronological. But where do the songs come from? and when did they originate? All evidence takes the ballads, the oldest comic ditties, and a few lyrical songs back as far as the Middle Ages. The medieval era itself, however, does not provide us with many direct written sources. Sparse fragments in various manuscripts reveal the antiquity of a few song types and genres still known today. They do not give us much to go on, however, and all kinds of evidence must be used to create an echo of the many violins; references in the sagas and chronicles; the Church's denunciations of worldly songs; representations in fresco paintings; old instruments, etc. The sixteenth- and seventeenth-century ballads could have been improvised by any smart lad familiar with the tradition, and elegiac lyrics composed by anybody with a little knowledge of the Danish echo of the era of chivalry and its literature. During the sixteenth century, which marks the transition from the Middle Ages to the modern era, and whose greatest event for Denmark was the Lutheran Reformation (1536), the eclipsed ballad and transient lyric poetry found asylum in the song books of ladies and gentlemen of high estate. The oldest of those song books is the renowned Heart Book of 1553–55. Certain of them were collections of ballads only, *e. g.* the famous folio manuscript called the Karen Brahe's Folio after a later owner and Anders Sørensen Vedel's *Et Hundrede Udvalgte Danske Viser* (One Hundred Selected Danish Songs), Northern Europe's first printed book of ballads, published in 1591. In such cases one may speak of a conscious antiquarian interest; but the texts are not necessarily on that account reliable representatives of their tradition. Such loyalty was alien to the scribes, who lived their material, took a hand in its composition, invented part of the story, and edited the result. In most of the manuscripts, however, ballads are heavily outnumbered by other types of sixteenth- and seventeenth-century songs. The song books of the aristocracy contain many departures from the older Danish tradition, but are of paramount importance, nevertheless, for our knowledge about Danish ballads in general. Our source index, accordingly, draws upon fifteen such manuscripts dating from 1550 to 1650 for references to a great many songs of all genres.

• Lyrics tended to be short-lived, especially chivalric lyrics; and we know too little about a written song tradition in the lower strata of society; only two or three surviving books of peasant songs bridge some of the gaps in our knowledge. Nevertheless, we owe the transmission of ballads even to the common people, its memory kept fresh by broadsides and by Vedel's edition, which was reprinted often in the seventeenth century. An enlarged selection prepared by Peder Syv appeared in a number of printings between 1695 and 1787. Broadsides – simple popular prints with one or a few songs or ballads – were printed down to our own day, with much newer material mixed in. Some of the new material was borrowed art poetry, religious songs especially, but most of it was aggressively commercial and dealt with topical events and popular sentimental subjects. An important song-milieu, the customs of village society, has been effective in preserving songs of the purely oral tradition.

• Archivists and men of letters, beginning about 1810, focused attention on folksongs, amassing great collections and subjecting the materials to scholarly analysis. The interest of these men was one of the early fruits of the Romantic movement. A. P. Berggreen, from 1840, Svend Grundtvig, after 1850, and Evald Tang Kristensen, from 1867, enlarged and accelerated the study of folksongs. Kristensen's colossal private collections centered on West Jutland. The Danish Folklore Archives, founded in 1905, used the Edison phonograph for recording, also in the Faroe Islands and Greenland. And nowadays, at a time when everyone thought that the Danish song tradition had died out, perceptive researchers equipped with modern tape recorders found unexpected material in both town and country. Thus, our chronological list of sources notes a series of songs recorded between 1837 and 1961 in addition to the broadsides and to various old prints made for other purposes than folk poetry.

• It is natural, then, that some of the classic ballads of this book are derived from recent recordings of the songs of the common people (Nos. 1, 3, 32, and 33). There are very late tape recordings of two items, 49 and 52. No. 49 was printed for the first time in the Danish edition which also included previously unquoted texts from original broadsides and from a peasant song book (Nos. 46, 48, 62, and 47). In other words, this book contains material first written, printed, or recorded at various times between the mid-thirteenth century and 1961 and dealing with songs that originated as early as 1200 and as late as 1800.

I • BALLADS. The ballad is the oldest of the ancient genres transmitted by popular singing and in other ways. The international term "ballad", during recent years, has gained acceptance in Scandinavian research as a substitute for the term *(gammel) folkevise,* "old folksong". Insufficient sources render the ancient history of the ballad nebulous, but it appears to have arrived in the North before 1200, directly or indirectly from France, possibly in company with the round dance and associated music; the Scandinavian ballads proved to have a stronger epic cast than the French song types with which they can best be compared. In subject matter, Nordic ballads are closer to English (and, later, German) ballads than to the French. The stanza forms are few; the couplet and the quatrain (see Nos. 2 and 3) are familiar to all readers of this book, for both forms are typical also of the English ballad. A strange variant, with repetitions, is seen in No. 8. A refrain is rarely lacking, never, in the true dance ballad; the esthetic effect of the refrain is great and unlike English ballads, it seldom consists of meaningless words; an interesting old feature of the refrain is seen in No. 77. This book gives more than usual emphasis to the refrain, which is repeated on each page; for the refrain, in the performance of the dance, is sung by everybody in chorus, whereas the leader alone chants the stanzas. The dance is still performed in this manner in the Faroe Islands; as a rule, the famous long refrains are abbreviated when the ballads are merely sung and not danced. Thus, it is possible that long refrains were part of the Danish *dance*-song tradition. However, the ballad was already on the wane when the Renaissance's new ways of dancing made it nonfunctional. Selections from its many types found their way to the common people, though many songs of the nobility never got out of the song books.

· Many of the characteristic features of the ballad depend, as a matter of fact, on the oral provenance and function of the song. The verse technique is simple; the treatment of weak syllables is free; links in the action, particularly transitions, are handled by stock phrases; the composition is simple, progressive, and episodic; dialogue is well developed, though situations with more than two speaking characters are hardly ever found; and the action is not involved. Descriptions occur, but are not natural to terse forward-moving action, and the cultural milieu is not described, for it is known to the audience (thus, it can be misunderstood by men of later traditions). There is almost never description of nature (see notes to Nos. 5 and 24), and man is pictured only through his speech and action. Nevertheless, human beings are not poorly described; the best of the ballads dig deeply. The poet and his audience find room for expression of mood in the refrain, often in a clever tension with the objective epic stanza sequence. Only gradually do lyrical terms enter the stanzas – "gradually" meaning both in later echoes of a certain song type and in newer songs generally, the expansion of lyric sentiment at the expense of straightforward narrative being a phenomenon typical of the late Middle Ages.

• The introductory lyrical stanza with which a small number of older ballads begin is lyrical (No. 26, expanded in No. 5). This type is called *stev-stem,* because the refrain (the *stev*) has grown out of the first stanza (see again No. 77). One of the favorite problems of research has been the antiquity of the stev-stem: Is it a vestige of a primitive lyrical folk poetry that existed in Scandinavia before the ballad was introduced? Or is it of later origin, added to the old ballads as a link in the lyrical development? Opinion today tends towards the latter verdict.

• The ballad is an all-Nordic matter, although its subdivisions are unevenly distributed. The subdivisions, from the time of Svend Grundtvig, have had such names as sorcery songs, legendary songs, historical songs, and hero songs. The rest – not having the contents indicated by those labels – is called songs of chivalry. It must be emphasized that all these groups belong to the same stratum, regardless of the world they describe or the circumstances from which they derive. The "hero songs" may be an exception.

1 • *Folklore* (Nature-mythical ballads, *trylleviser,* DgF II). This group within the many hundreds of Nordic ballads is of the greatest value for our understanding of medieval man. Ancient international motifs are included in the themes; even a ballad like No. 2, known all over Europe, seems almost devoid of perspective in time and space, by comparison with the main motif of No. 7. The folklore elements – strange creatures in nature, transformations, ghosts, rune sorcery – are never used as in fairy tales, which often bring tribulations to their characters but almost always finish by obliging the wishful thinking of their audience. In the ballads, nature is the expression of the unknown. There is a possible two-fold explanation for this: Beyond the tilled fields and rose gardens of the medieval world lay Nature, unconquered by man and his mind. Its real and

"imagined" dangers (as they are grandiosely called) were personified by creatures of the ballads. At the same time, the action and trappings in some of the ballads are symbolic interpretations, attempts to suggest wild, ungrasped dimensions of man's soul and fate. Thus, the bridge in No. 1 is a symbol of fright and of a transition, and the ensnaring tones in No. 4 an erotic symbol. Axel Olrik, Ernst Frandsen, and, lately, Villy Sørensen have, with varying emphasis, tried to establish a chronological thread from songs in which the evocation of mood is uppermost and the story almost impersonally schematic (Nos. 1 and 2) to more individualized songs where the forcefulness of nature symbols is attenuated but still real (No. 4), and, ultimately, to later songs where the poet is a free, creative spirit, and the runes, transformations, etc., are only poetic conventions. The best pieces of this group of ballads present us with deeply sensed human values; they are neither Christian nor pagan in orientation. In them, as in many ballads without supernatural elements, man, for good or ill, is at the mercy of forces he cannot control. Ideas of predestination and – later – chance are only adumbrated. The attitude of the ballads toward reality has varied greatly. The best nature-mythical ballads were reduced by Orthodoxy and Rationalism as being free and perhaps sinful imagination, but are now considered as an expression of a mysterious reality, so mysterious that it could not be expressed otherwise by medieval man, and hardly by ourselves.

2 · *Christianity* (Legendary ballads, *legendeviser,* DgF II and IX). This group, small in Denmark, is separated here from Chapter 1. The myth about St. Olav (Norway's saint king, d. 1030), St. Stephen, and the praying soul of the child has little connection with ordinary experience or with church dogma. This holds true of the sorcery songs, too, but in quite another way. The legendary songs are meaningless without the Christian background and often represent "Christian superstition," whereas the sorcery songs perpetuate heathen folklore and basic human concepts. Both groups, however, afford insight into the mixed spiritual ideas of medieval times; and the legendary songs are deserving of our interest in spite of their sparseness. (See also Chapter 8).

3 · *Kings and Nobles* (Historical ballads, *historiske viser,* DgF III). These songs, of course, have attracted historians as well as other scholars, who occupy themselves with the ballad for different reasons. Their historicity has encountered scepticism, but Svend Grundtvig believed, nevertheless, that generally they coincided in date with their subject matter. The end result of discussion over the past hundred years is the view that each ballad must be judged individually. Thus, we can detect a shift in their development from pure invention with haphazard use of historic names, first to more or less accurate accounts of actual events of a certain time, and then to unquestionably contemporaneous compositions (such as Nos. 14, 17, 18). The authenticity of these last cannot be taken for granted merely because of their great age, for the poets were often poorly informed or directly partisan (sometimes to the point of being bought-and-paid-for propagandists). However, that in itself is of special source value as an expression of a certain historical opinion. Ballads dealing with important "historically known" personalities have for ages been called "historical ballads"; but many knightly songs undoubtedly encompass real but forgotten persons and events, and are therefore more "historical" than ballads of kings and heroes. One common attribute ought to govern our reading of them: they all are poetry. Nevertheless, this edition comments more fully upon even these ballads than did the Danish edition, because the historical ballads have been of great importance for the general concepts of the persons concerned; not only belletristic works but also the works of certain historians and their reflection in school text books have contributed to this.

4 · *Saga and Myth* (Hero ballads, *kæmpeviser,* DgF I). Grundtvig put this group first in his source publication because he regarded it as the most ancient, taken over directly from the oldest strata of traditions about King Dietrich of Bern (Theodoric of Ravenna), Charlemagne, the House of the Volsungs (the same as the German Nibelung cycle), etc. The same subjects are found in West Nordic tradition: the Volsung themes, for example, in the Elder Edda. Grundtvig took energetic part in polemics about these subjects toward the end of his life (see DgF IV), and in the eyes of posterity,

emerged second best. The hero songs are now regarded as medieval works, originating in (western) Norway on the basis of relatively late written versions of the old mythological themes. One group of Norwegian troll songs is related to the late Icelandic fairy-tale sagas: the fairy-tale features of the hero ballads are particularly conspicuous in these. The episodic composition characteristic of the ballad has often led to these long poems being divided into sections. The naive, often burlesque fairy-tale ballad unrelated to reality, though often lacking the refinement and coherence of the East Scandinavian chivalric or sorcery ballad, has many points of interest both in form and in content.

5 • *Love and Death.* 6 • *Humor and Sadness* (Ballads of chivalry, *ridderviser,* DgF IV–IX). Love and feudal fight are the most constant motifs of the knightly ballads. They are pitched in many different keys, which have a certain relation to their age. Nos. 24–27 are old, and in them evil fortune reigns supreme. But No. 30, despite all its misery, is made of softer stuff and seems modern in its suggestion of conflict. The notes sounded in Nos. 32–34 are lighter, and 35–37 belong to a later outlook and lyrical idiom, as visible here as in the latest sorcery songs. The old, solid epic poetry with a possible base in ancient tradition has been undermined here; these ballads rest on the boundary of the DgF area and for this reason should be included in a selection such as this, which also presents their fully lyrical relatives.

• The knightly ballads reflect the milieu in which they were created. Historical and cultural accounts of the Danish Middle Ages often build a mosaic with ballads as the chief source for chapters on customs and habits, housing and dress, feudal structure, festivals, etc. Many an opus by a poet from our golden age of early nineteenth-century Romanticism has a *mise-en-scène* drawn from folk ballads or, in works with non-medieval themes, at least a folksong idiom based on appropriate features from balladry. Ballads change with time so often and in so many psychological, social, and material areas, that their variations and evolution are considerations as important to our study as their lost original forms; we must remember, furthermore, that we are looking at poetry. Most Danes read

Romantic masterpieces on medieval themes before they read ballads; for instance, Henrik Hertz's *Svend Dyrings Hus* (1837) and Christian Winther's epic *Hjortens Flugt* (Flight of the Deer) (1856) are still living literature. But the grand culture of chivalry depicted in books like these is only an aspect and not the most important of the stark reality of the medieval Denmark revealed to us by the ballad in its stylized way. Many of the concepts, usages, and properties of the Middle Ages seem to have shifted in meaning in later times, for example in Peder Syv's songbook (1695), in which there is a list of "old and peculiar" words. Some of the words are still quite common to us, but others now belong in a glossary of Romantic poetry. They are encountered in Peder Syv's book as archaic expressions which need explanation, without necessarily having had poetic import in the time that created the songs and lived with the elements described in them.

II · HUMOR. 7 · *Jocular songs (skæmteviser).* Comic songs are found in all the forms and ways of tradition, indicated by the stanza construction of our samples and the index of sources. They cover the same chronological range as the other chapters. Comic songs, in the past, have not been a separate classification, but have been merged with other songs according to their structure and chronology. There is inherent justification for tabulating them this way, but the chief reason for this practice is that some editors and publishers have been too dainty to focus on these often vulgar and bawdy songs. In numerous cases, however, they refer to priests, students, laborers, and other social strata unknown to the ballad; and their relation to the ballad is often satirical. Both characteristics suggest a later age. But other types, though very old (No. 44), are still alive, including some humorous pieces in DgF. The comic song has perpetuated the song-accompanied Danish dance for the longest time (in our century on the island Manø).

III · LATER SONGS ("Echoes", *efterklang*). The term *(Kæmpevisens) Efterklang,* "echo (of the ballad)", invented by Svend Grundtvig for later songs, is not really a proper one. Not only does the word suggest that this group is later in date than the ballads (which is more or less true), but also that in some way it represents attenuation of the ballad (only true of a small group that preserves the chorus without any epic structure or content). The term covers a great variety of song types. The repertoire was originally presented, developed, and elucidated in indexes by Grundtvig and The Danish Folklore Archives (and, printed, in Nils Schiørring's exhaustive study of 1950, see page 295). In our Chapter 12 we have added songs that Schiørring has not taken into consideration (Nos. 69, 70, 72). The criteria for "echo songs" take us far away from the ballad to: (1) songs in the style of the ballad but without its meters; (2) derivations from the German *Volkslied*, itself a heterogeneous concept; (3) popular broadsides; (4) festivity and annual-procession songs; in other words, they are classified by form, origin, popularity, and function! These classifications are further complicated by attempts to place the songs socially (compare the notes to Chapters 10 and 12). These categories are applied to a great number and variety of types: (a) spiritual songs, including church-festival songs; (b) worldly songs of every shade from pure epic to pure lyric; (c) historical songs, partly political, partly biographical, and partly direct narrative. The diversity is not less conspicuous in regard to rhythm and melody. The oldest of these songs were possibly born as early as 1500, the youngest in this book as late as 1800. Broadside publishing was well established by 1800, and the genre has survived until today. To a certain degree, it presents its own special problems to the researcher.

• Though the sixteenth century is the only period of overlapping between the ballad and the echo, it is important to consider them as parallels as far as transmission is concerned. Though the ballad to an increasing degree is displaced by later songs it is still important to stress that upper-class song books *and* broadsides *and* popular oral tradition are composed by ballads *and* humorous songs *and* echoes; the ratio of mixture varies with each individual case, but it is organic. Often, still other ingredients are added, namely hymns and art poetry; see the annotated edition *Gamle danske viser,* 1939 ff, by Arthur Arnholtz, Nils Schiørring, and Finn Viderø, especially parts 1 and 2, in which we can observe the outer and inner borderlines crossing ours in an intriguing way.

8 · *Creed and Superstition.* This chapter unites quite different and very interesting songs, all of which must be examined in the light of Christianity, even though some of them (*i. e.,* No. 48) express "religious" ideas of a lower caliber. Nos. 50–51 have been placed here because their theme is the Church. The last representatives of the historical ballad and its successors were apt to become as dry as mere chronicles (Nos. 18 og 19 are moving and droll exceptions to the rule). Many of the songs about events and people require too much commentary to be read profitably; and on the whole they enjoy less popularity in the folk tradition. The songs of the seasons are interesting for their practical role and their popularity; also other groups are represented. They all contributed to edification, instruction, and entertainment. No. 49 has not been printed hitherto, although it is known in other versions. No. 47 is known only in this version, which has been taken from one of the few peasant song books and symbolizes the way in which the folk song survived though declassed by the contempt for it during the time of Holberg.

9 · *Romances, romanviser.* Svend Grundtvig seems to have created the term which encompasses a group of ballads in DgF VIII, whose popular center was DgF 475, *Aslag Tordsøn og skjøn Valborg (Axel og Valborg)* in 200 quatrains. Some of these ballads have themes exhibiting parallels with the popular Continental cycles of legendary hero ballads. This late group of ballads slides smoothly into the echo's group of novel songs without a refrain. In both cases, the narrative of the novel songs flows in a broader stream than is permitted by the classical ballad's well-balanced episodes and individual stanzas. Mawkish sentimentality intrudes into the echo novel songs, which were often translations and which became highly popular through broadsides. This is especially true of No. 53, an international type, which in popularity tops the list of novel songs in Germany and Denmark even today. Our other two samples belong to an older tradition, but No. 54 has also been popular here, though the scene is alien to Denmark.

10 • *Stories about Love.* This title ought to be understood in a broad popular sense, for we have here the most beloved narrative echo types. Nils Schiørring, who records only versions with melodies, has as many as thirty tunes to some of these songs, a number of which are still alive. This is not true of Nos. 56 and 57, both of which are partly lyrical and chivalric, like most songs in the following chapter (compare Chapter 12), but many melodies exist for the top favorites, Nos. 58 and 59. Chronologically and stylistically these are marginal items in the present anthology. A song like No. 59 is an epic guideline to the broadside versifications of the nineteenth century; songs like this are forerunners of our present entertainment industry, and thus are receiving a fairer evaluation by sociologists and folklorists than by literary and music critics.

11 • *The Woman Worshipped.* Nos. 61–70 represent the Danish Renaissance lyric, whose imprint was already seen in Nos. 56 and 57 and which invaded the ballad genre with results like those in Nos. 35–37. Traditionally, the lyric has narrower time limits than many of the songs already mentioned, for normally, it has not survived to be included in the collections of the nineteenth century; while still alive, however, it belonged to two often-mentioned traditions, the songs of the nobles and the broadsides. The genre as such, together with many of the individual poems, came from Germany with echoes of chivalry that spread across the map from France, and a certain monotony, lack of expression, and lack of imagery cannot be denied. We are deeply in need of older sources for elucidation of this genre's history. Is the reason for its stiffness the fact that the lyric, as we know it, already had a tradition of which we are not aware, and had become exhausted? Or, is this type the naive herald of a new outlook breaking down into abstraction and cliché, because of its youthful and touching lack of self-confidence? These two theories are propounded by Ernst Frandsen and F. J. Billeskov Jansen respectively. Swedish research (Karl-Ivar Hildeman) supports the cause of lyric flow in the Middle Ages, but, in the main, this genre cannot be so old that Billeskov Jansen's characterization of it loses its validity.

· No 60 is key to the present debate on this subject because it was put in writing before 1500 and is clearly built on troubadour conventions. That, in itself, may justify our placement of the poem, which, though we would not have omitted it from this collection in any case, would otherwise have been relegated to the appendix (see Notes). Further, No. 67, with its learned, mystic images, falls outside this scheme, unlike No. 68, which is broader in form. Their unmistakably shared heartbeat of personal fight for life, however, binds these poems together against the contrasting background of the ordinary lyric of the time. It should be mentioned that this anthologist is responsible for quite a few titles in these chapters. The titles of Nos. 60, 67, and 68 especially, are based on hypothesis, not on established fact. (See Notes).

12 · *The Woman Longing.* This small chapter is heterogeneous. In addition to the already mentioned No. 68, the precious No. 69 (comparable to the pseudo-ballad No. 35) and the hearty No. 70, three small songs are presented from the much later peasant tradition. They are connected with the three old texts only by their subjects, although No. 73 possibly is an offshoot from the same tradition. These two groups have in common their anonymous dissemination, in manuscripts and in peasant tradition respectively. But each distinctly carries the imprint of its social milieu, almost like the two pairs of songs in Chapter 10. Nos. 72 and 73 have been translated from better texts than those used in the Danish edition. (See Notes).

IV · ADDENDUM. V · NOTES AND INDEXES. We have nothing of interest to mention about the small collection of supplementary material gathered together in our Part IV. In Part V, attention is directed to the literary index on page 294. Our short introduction and rather extensive notes are supposed to open up, rather than bar, the road to annotated source publications and broader presentations of the themes. Topics include esthetic evaluation of the songs and elucidation of their musical relationships, as well as more specialized matters.

THE MELODIES. Any exposition of the melodies of the ballads suffers, because there are still fewer contemporaneous sources for them than for the text. The identification signal of the Danish radio, the renowned melody of No. 74-c, for several reasons provides no answer to some of the most burning questions that one might wish to put to a true melody of the Middle Ages. Only a handful of bona fide ballad tunes had been preserved by 1810. We are a little better off for post-medieval melodies, particularly since Nils Schiørring has reviewed the motley material rather thoroughly. The past 150 years, however, have furnished all the song groups with an impressive number of melodies, and modern technical equipment is, of course, of especial value here because written music offers much less of the "reality" than the written text. • Things being what they are, nothing more than supposition may be presented about the oldest forms of Nordic *ballad melodies.* We shall mention here an old bone of contention: some authorities regarded melodic features alien to the musical ear of the nineteenth century as relics of old Nordic music forms, about which little was or is known. Others reasoned that the Gregorian song had influenced these melodies to a great degree. Church music, undeniably, must have been among the earliest influences of the Continent's musical superculture on the distant Scandinavian countries. The "Gregorian" theory became authoritative in this century on the basis of Thomas Laub's artistic work with the best of the melodies and his valuable essays on the subject. Laub's contribution in this sphere appeared at the beginning of the century, at the same time as his pioneering work on the Danish church hymn, and brought about a higher understanding of older tunes and melodic forms. • It is acknowledged today that the pastoral-wordly question (*i. e.,* imported or homespun) is not quite so simple. Interdisciplinary cooperation between research in medieval music and comparative ethnomusicology has shown that certain formal and structural types are broadly extended in both time and in space, and that the practice and theory of church music (to place the words in the right sequence) did not develop without influence from the flowering of worldly medieval music. What resembles modal usage in our melodies may have been influenced by it, but, on the other hand, may have sprung from the same roots – or the resemblance may have been caused by the sharing of well-nigh universal principles of music structure. And, although recorded at a late date, ballad melodies may contain features of great antiquity, possibly older than Christianity and older than the entrance of modal church song into the daily life of Scandinavia. At the same time it must be stressed that, just as the stanza form defines the ballad, regardless of the similarity of themes with other poetry forms or folklore, the origin of the ballad-melody form cannot be determined apart from the importation of the poetic genre. What is more natural than to suppose that conflict arose between imported and the native – just as, later on, changes in melody and formation of new melodies come about as the result of changing musical vogues?

• The accumulation of material itself created problems. The men who wrote down the melodies had generally no special qualifications for the assignment beyond a more or less general interest in music. Their method, dictated by their Classic-Romantic frame of reference, was, at the irrevocable moment of recording, to notate the sung melody, according to our conventional scale allowing very little possibility of catching deviant tones and rhythms or of determining whether such deviations were incidental mistakes or characteristic features of folk music. It may be a consolation that even the most advanced modern research on folk music has not overcome the problem of deciding between a notation that, despite more or less intricacy, is at least readable, and a graphic film-tape reproduction of the song's acoustic details. The main thing is that ballad and dance are so intimately connected that the original melodies must have had broad similarities with those preserved: the invariable framework, the free use of varying numbers of weak syllables, the highly inflective underlining. To put it briefly, the relatively easy and simple elements in the musical structure may belong to the stable features of the genre.

• The *comic and echo songs* created in free ballad forms naturally followed the existing music, especially its younger strata dominated by major chords. Of course, there were never as many melodies as there were ballads. There was extensive interchange inside this great but metrically homogeneous repertoire, and the form of the

refrain was a deciding factor. According to the custom that still exists in the Faroe Islands, the singing of the ballad began with the uttering of its refrain; it has had a function similar to that of the melody reference in a modern songbook without music.
· The situation is different in a variety of ways with respect to the stock of melodies used for the majority of the echo songs with the abundant new stanza forms. It may seem peculiar that *melodies of hymns* occupied a large domain here, not only in relation to biblical and morality poems and procession songs, but also in relation to political and personal songs. These groups are strongly dominated by the hymn and ballad music. However, this is not strange, considering that the dividing line between pastoral and non-pastoral was vaguer during early times than later on, both musically and otherwise (see Nos. 57 and 79). Further, the versifiers of the time had to use known melodies to some extent. Thus, a comprehensive book like Schiørring's must, although primarily musicological, create a synopsis by division according to text genres – as folk song editors have always done, be they conversant with music or not.
· The worldly songs, our Chapters 9–12, are preponderately worldly in their melodies, and German influence in both text and melody is as easy to detect as in the novel song and the erotic lyric. Many of the texts and melodies of these songs are known only in comparatively late versions, and their original melody grouping is difficult to discern. But, by ascertaining or surmising their connection with their German ancestors, we gain a comparatively solid basis for evaluating these melody genres in general. Searching through the innumerable complexities of the material, Schiørring – whose registration is referred to here – reached the major conclusion "that the melody material of the echo songs is relatively loyal to tradition and clearly typical, century after century".

AFTER EFFECTS. Both the ballad and the later folksong were, however, put on the defensive, as time went on, despite their tenacity. There was no lack of interest among leading cultural circles in re-establishing the folksong. The composers C. E. F. Weyse and A. P. Berggreen experimented with folksongs in piano settings, winning considerable popularity; and every Danish song anthology had and still has its samples of folksong. Thomas Laub went his own way and created beautiful unison versions of the tunes, based on his conception of their affinity to modal church music. But none of them won out in their attempts to preserve folk music. It was not possible to put up decisive resistance against the inroads of artistic music, especially among the populations of the towns. The club song, from the late eighteenth century, the romance from about 1800, the patriotic song in the spirit of N. F. S. Grundtvig of the 1840s, the typical Danish nature lyric of a later date, the revival of the musical repertoire of these genres by the seminary movement – and the musical crisis of our age, which is strangely song-poor despite the entertainment industry, tell the story. The old collectively functioning genres have lost most of their purpose, although they still have a place and acceptance in our school system. (For further elucidation we shall refer to Karl Clausen, *Dansk folkelig sang gennem 150 år* (1958), and Niels Martin Jensen, *Den danske romance 1800–1850 og dens musikalske forudsætninger* (1964). That new collectors and new methods of collecting have shown unexpected life in the old popular genres within certain circles, is, of course, surprising and gratifying, but does not alter the fact that these genres have disappeared from cultural life. Time will show to which extent traditional songs *of quality* will be revived by the 'folk-song movement' of this decade.

It is, therefore, well to remember, that the importance of the ballads since their rediscovery about two hundred years ago has been limited neither to private enjoyment by singers and readers nor to contributions by scholarly researchers to the twelve feet of shelf space that books on Danish folksong occupy. For the ballads and their tunes have inspired poets, composers, and illustrators. Before 1800 folksong had already provided the nation with its literary and musical conception of the "romance". The historical songs colored popular understanding of the Middle Ages, not least through B. S. Ingemann's idealized and (in a national sense) fertile historical novels written in the 1820s and 30s. Musical compositions also drew material, although not always melodies, from the world of the ballad. Examples that may be mentioned include J. L. Heiberg's musical play *Elverhøj* of 1828, N. W. Gade's 1845 choral composition *Elverskud* (se notes to Nos. 2 and 3), and the only two operas of the nineteenth century that have stayed alive until the middle of our own, *Liden Kirsten,* by the two friends J. P. Hartmann and Hans Christian Andersen, 1846, and Peter Heise's Marsk Stig opera *Drot og Marsk,* 1877 (libretto by Christian Richardt). Certain ballads and ballad characters have attracted poet after poet – Agnete and the Merman, Aage and Else, Ebbe Skammelsen, Valdemar and Tove. We have thus in this century, six Ebbe Skammelsen dramas, most of them, however, by obscure or unknown authors; the most important are Valdemar Rørdam's *Grønlandsfærd,* 1912, in which Ebbe is on an expedition to Greenland, away from the milieu of his Danish estate, and another by Sonja Hauberg, 1945, in which the brothers are respectively a soldier and a member of the home guard during a world war. Also general and special metrical forms, and refrain effects, have been cultivated by poets during two hundred years.

• It is not just in Denmark, however, that the Danish folksong has put its imprint on the arts. The Danish ballads were also read abroad. The version of *The Elf-Shot* presented here as No. 3 was already read by Herder in Peder Syv's collection. He published it in his *Volkslieder* in 1778–79, and thus gave Goethe the inspiration for *Erlkönig;* further, Herder's own translation became part and parcel of German folk tradition. Wilhelm Grimm's first book was one hundred old Danish hero ballads: *Altdänische Heldenlieder,* 1811, written in intimate cooperation with Nyerup, and in itself of great importance for the latter's ballad book. In addition to the English translators numerous Germans and two Frenchmen should be noted. The indirect effect cannot be evaluated precisely.

• Since the pre-Romantic era, Danish and Nordic ballads have trickled out to scholars and poets, coloring their view of Northern Europe and inspiring part of their writings, although to a lesser degree than the West-Nordic Edda and saga. The ballad, the *folkevise,* created as East Scandinavia's most original contribution in the Middle Ages and never wholly forgotten, thus – together with the later song, which is less well known to leading cultural circles – make important contributions to one's understanding of Danish poetry, Danish history, and Danish character.

Erik Dal

I · BALLADS

1 · FOLKLORE

1 THE POWER OF MUSIC
Recording from West Jutland by P. K. Toksvig, 1872

Sir Peter rides into the quad,
fair maiden meets him there so sad.
– My dearest sweetheart, why grievest thou so deeply?

"Grievest thou for either saddle or steed,
or grievest thou that thou art betrothed to me?"

"No, I don't grieve for saddle or steed
and neither that I am betrothed to thee.

But I grieve for the stream so wide,
for in it lie my sisters five.

5 · In it lie my sisters five,
it is foretold I shall lie at their side."

"Harken, fair maiden, neither sorrow nor pine,
with you shall ride twelve squires of mine.

Four in front and four at the rear
and two men on each side."

They came to the river bridge at the sluice,
there reared the steed on four golden shoes.

And thirty nails with gold a-gleam;
fair maiden fell into the raging stream.

10 · Sir Peter he speaks to his page so small:
"Go fetch me my golden horn from my hall."
– My dearest sweetheart, why grievest thou so deeply?

He raised the horn and artfully blew,
no bird did move in birch or yew.

He blew the bark off linden and fir,
the horns off cows, the antlers off deer.

The merman came up on strand,
the maiden he held in his hand.

"Here is your bride so fair of form,
pray, rest thou now thy golden horn."

15 · "No, I shan't rest my golden horn,
before thou fetchest her sisters five."

The merman came up on strand,
five maidens he held in his hand.

"And here thou hast her sisters five,
pray, rest thou now thy golden horn."

"No, I shan't rest my golden horn,
before thou fetchest thy finest gold."

The merman came up from the waters beneath,
the finest gold he held in his teeth.

20 · "And there thou hast thy finest gold,
pray rest thou now thy accursèd horn."

21 · His valiant sword Sir Peter drew,
he fell on the merman whom he slew.
– My dearest sweetheart, why grievest thou so deeply?

2 THE ELF-SHOT
Peter Syv's augmented edition, 1695, of Vedel's Ballad Book

Many ride, erect and red,
still next morning, ill and dead.

So widely Sir Oluf does ride,
his wedding guests to invite.
– *So blithely they tread the dance in the meadow.*

The dance is trod by five, by ten,
the elfin king's daughter waves to him.

"Welcome, Sir Oluf, thy haste let be,
bide for a while and dance with me."

"Neither I dare to, nor I may,
tomorrow is my wedding day."

5 · "Listen, Sir Oluf, thou dance with me,
two buckskin boots shall I give to thee.

Two buckskin boots, so well they fit
with golden spurs on, thou wilst get.

Listen, Sir Oluf, thou dance with me,
a shirt of silk shall I give to thee.

A shirt of silk so white and groomed,
my mother she bleached it by the shine of the moon."

"Neither I dare to, nor I may,
tomorrow is my wedding day."

10 · "Listen, Sir Oluf, thou dance with me,
a bushel of gold shall I give to thee."

"A bushel of gold I'll have, maybe,
but I don't dare to dance with thee."
– So blithely they tread the dance in the meadow.

"And wilst thou not tread the dance with me,
plague and sickness shall follow thee."

She smote him then across the back,
never was he harder struck.

She lifted him onto his steed so red:
"Ride home and see thy beloved maid."

15 · When he came to the castle gate,
there was his mother waiting so late.

"Listen, Sir Oluf, my dearest son,
why is thy cheek so white and wan?"

"My cheek may well be wan and white,
for I have been at the elfin princess' side."

"Listen, Sir Oluf, my son so fine,
what shall I tell the young bride of thine?"

"That I went to the woods and bogs
to train my horse and drill my dogs."

20 · Early that morning when sun came out
the bride arrived with the wedding crowd.

They poured the mead and they poured the wine.
"Where is Sir Oluf, bridegroom of mine?"

"Sir Oluf he rode to the woods and bogs
to train his horse and drill his dogs."

She raised the cover so red,
there was Sir Oluf, and he was dead.
– *So blithely they tread the dance in the meadow.*

Early that morning when sun came out,
three bodies there were in Sir Oluf's house.

25 · Sir Oluf and his beloved maid,
his mother, too, from sorrow dead.
– *So blithely they tread the dance in the meadow.*

Remark: It was thought, and ordinary people believe it still, that an elfin king existed at Stevens, and that no other king was allowed to come there; but Christian IV, Frederik III, Christian V had been there a few times and so they killed this notion . . . The daughter of the elfin king was called the elfin lady or the elfin woman and lured the menfolk, and the el or elfin lured the womenfolk; these were very common phantoms of earlier times, about whom little is heard since the spread of the shining light of the gospel. People also talk about elfin books, which they at times gave to those whom they loved, out of which they could predict all sorts of things to come. – He who was seduced by them, was called elfin-wild, and it was said about them that the elfin lay with them. But in this song Sir Oluf is mistreated and elfin-struck, because he would not be led astray by the elfins and take part in the elfin dance with these elfins.

3 THE ELF HILL
Recording from West Jutland by Evald Tang Kristensen, 1868

My father gave me saddle and horse
to ride into court upon;
my mother gave me cushions blue
that I should sleep thereon.
– *Never since first I saw them.*

I rested my head at the elfin hill,
my eyes they were heavy with sleep,
then came to me the maidens three,
they wanted to talk to me.
– *Never since first I saw them.*

One stroked my cheek so wan and white,
another whispered in my ear:
"Oh, get thee up, my handsome youth,
and tread the dance with us here.

Yes, we shall teach you runes and books,
also to read and write;
the dragon of gold at Northernhall
from the land you shall chase away.

5 • The dragon of gold at Northernhall
from the land you shall chase away.
So get thee up, my handsome youth,
if you with us will stay."

And one began to sing a song,
the far most beautiful one;
the roaring stream became quiet then
that before was wont to run.

The roaring stream became quiet then
that before was wont to run;
and all the small fish who dwelt in the stream
wiggled their fins in fun.

Yes, all the small fish who dwelt in the stream
began to play with their tail;
and all the small birds who were asleep
began to sing in the dale.

And all the while the handsome youth
sat resting on his spear.
"And if you will not speak with us,
then badly you shall fare.
– *Never since first I saw them.*

10 · Yes, listen, listen, handsome youth,
if you with us won't speak,
then surely spear and sharpest knife
shall put your heart to sleep."

If fortune hadn't favored me,
and the cock not sung his lays,
I'd never have escaped from the elfin hill
and from the elfin maids.

12 · Thus counsel I, all handsome youths,
wherever you may ride,
take not the road to the elfin hill
and sleep not on its side.
– *Never since first I saw them.*

4 THE KNIGHT'S RUNES
Karen Brahe's Folio Manuscript, 1583

Sir Peter and Sir Oluf they sat one day
and spoke many a word so light and gay.
– *Yonder my sweetheart awakens under the linden tree.*

Sir Peter he swore by his faith and said
that he could lure so many a maid.

"In all the world there isn't a maid
whom by my runes I couldn't bait."

Sir Oluf pounded his hand on the boards:
"Sir Peter, stop using that kind of words.
– *Yonder my sweetheart awakens under the linden tree.*

5 • I have betrothed me a maiden demure
whom with your runes you shall never lure."

"Now I will wager my gold so red,
that I shall lure this maid to my bed."

His gold-harp Sir Peter began to play,
fair Kirsten heard it from far away.

Sir Peter blew on his golden horn,
home to fair Kirsten the tones were borne.

Fair Kirsten listened in charmed delight:
"I wonder if I should go yonder tonight."

10 • She stood for a long time musingly:
"None of my maidens must follow me."

Fair Kirsten and her little dog
went by themselves across the bog.

She tapped on the door with her neckpiece skin:
"Arise, Sir Peter, and let me in.

Sir Peter, open and let me through,
I yearn so sorely for speaking to you."

"Even with all this yearning by you,
this evening to me you shan't get through.

15 • I should be glad to open the door
but for Sir Oluf, your master and lord.

And even if you hold me for ever dear,
for us Sir Oluf is far too near."
– *Yonder my sweetheart awakens under the linden tree.*

"Arise, Sir Peter, and let me in,
the dew lies wet on my neckpiece skin."

"And lies the dew on your neckpiece skin,
then turn that out that before was in."

"If you won't let me into your room,
let some of your squires see me home."

20 · "Tonight the moon is nice and clear,
all by yourself you will have to fare.

Tonight the moon is clear in the sky,
all by yourself you must find your way."

Fair Kirsten and her little dog
went by themselves across the bog.

The highway Kirsten decided to use,
the hidden trail Sir Oluf chose.

When she came to the castle gate,
Sir Oluf stood there at the hour so late.

25 · "Welcome, fair Kirsten, from field and bower,
where have you been at this late hour?"

"I walked for a while down at the brook,
at the small flowers I wanted to look.

I looked at the flowers along the creek,
the fairest of them I wanted to pick.

I saw roses, red and white,
the sight of them was a sweet delight."
– *Yonder my sweetheart awakens under the linden tree.*

"This walk tonight and others alike
will surely us both with witchcraft strike.

30 • This walk tonight and others akin,
fair Kirsten, I beg you, don't do it again."

Fair Kirsten sat upright in her bed
with sorrow in mind and a heart that bled.

And then, when Sir Oluf had gone to sleep,
out of the bed fair Kirsten did creep.

Shame on Sir Peter's golden harp,
that charms so many an honest bride.

Shame on Sir Peter's gold-horn so red,
it lures so many an honest maid!

35 • Fair Kirsten drew from her sleeve the knife:
"With honor I shall take my life."

Sir Oluf awoke, dismayed and awed,
he swam in his dear Kirsten's blood.

Against the ground he pitted the hilt,
and by the sword his blood was spilt.

O, all young men, this is my plea,
tempt not the wife who loves purity.

39 • They both had to die, it was grief and woe;
and later Sir Peter died by the sword.
– *Yonder my sweetheart awakens under the linden tree.*

5 THE FEATHERED MAIDEN
Svaning's Manuscript I, about 1580

I've often been in a forest
so far away at the fiord,
in it grow the fairest trees
of which you ever heard.
– So wins a youth his maiden.

In it are the fairest trees,
both linden and willow grow;
in it gambol the beautiful deer
that you call stag and doe.

In it gambol both stag and doe,
and other fair beasts there be;
in it sings a small nightingale
in a green linden tree.

That he heard, Nilaus Erlandsen,
who always went hunting about.
He saddled his steed with the golden-red shoes,
rode yonder to seek it out.

5 · Yonder rode Nilaus Erlandsen,
so bootlessly did he fare:
there he stayed for three whole days,
the bird he couldn't snare.

Then he put snares on all the trees
where the bird was used to sit;
the small bird used her eyes so well,
he couldn't garner it.

He put the snares on every path
where the bird was used to dwell;
he couldn't catch the little bird,
she used her eyes so well.

And he took his axe in hand,
he wanted to fell the tree;
entered the man who owned the wood
with a spear so threateningly.
– *So wins a youth his maiden.*

"If you cut my ancestral wood,
if you do me this tort,
I promise you, Nilaus Erlandsen,
that you shall suffer for 't."

10 • Quoth the beautiful maiden then
from high above the tors:
"Lad, if you listen to my advice,
then shall the bird be yours.

Harken to me, my handsome lad,
and listen to my advice:
if you haven't some uncooked meat,
away the wild bird flies."

He cut the flesh out of his chest,
hung it on the linden tree;
she seemed to like it and fluttered her wings,
the flesh she wanted to keep.

And when the little nightingale
took hold of the bloody meat,
she changed into the fairest maid
who set on earth her feet.

In her silken sark she stood
under the linden tree;
and the knight took her in his arms,
they spoke of their agony.

15 · The knight he took her in his arms
and patted her cheek so white:
"Tell me, dearest sweetheart of mine,
who caused you all your plight?"
– So wins a youth his maiden.

"Playing with lilies and roses in bloom
I sat in my father's hall;
and my stepmother entered the room,
that didn't please her at all.

She changed me into a nightingale,
bid me to fly out here;
my seven maidens she changed into wolves
and bid them the bird to tear."

The maid stood under the linden tree,
loosened her beautiful hair;
her seven maids came running along,
and seven wolves they were.

19 · And now has Nilaus Erlandsen
recovered from anguish and harm;
and now he sleeps so happily,
hugged by his maiden's arm.
– So wins a youth his maiden.

6 THE BURIED MOTHER
Recording from West Jutland by Evald Tang Kristensen, 1869

Fair Ellen she rests with God in the sky
– in the coppice –
and there she heard her little ones cry.
– In the coppice wither the roses.

Fair Ellen she went before His throne:
– *in the coppice* –
"O Lord, may I go to my children home?"
– *In the coppice wither the roses.*

"Of course, you may home to your children go,
but this time you may not cause any woe."

Fair Ellen walked quietly in the dark,
but all the small dogs began to bark.

5 • And when she came to the castle gate,
there stood her oldest daughter at the hour so late.

"O, welcome, dear mother, you look like a dead;
you're now so pale who were rosy red."

"Of course I am pale and not rosy red,
I have lain in my grave, so long been dead."

They came to the door and their road was blocked,
for it was sealed with a cross and locked.

And when she couldn't go through the door,
she entered the house through a wee mousehole.

10 • Fair Ellen walked quietly 'cross the floor,
it filled her children with joy to the core.

And one she brushed, another she plaited,
her oldest daughter she mildly berated:

"Your brothers and sisters you thus must treat,
you know full well that their mother is dead."

She laid the youngest to suck at her breast,
with mighty vigor the milk was blessed.

Fair Ellen she went to the bedroom door,
– in the coppice –
'twas blocked by cross and lock as before.
– In the coppice wither the roses.

15 · And when she couldn't go through the door,
she entered the room through a wee mousehole.

"Arise, Sir Peter, and speak to me;
how have you acted and how may you be?

Left I not gold enough so red,
my little ones shouldn't cry for bread?

Left I not candles by the score,
my children should be in the dark no more?

Left I not covers without a flaw,
my children shouldn't sleep on straw?

20 · Again I surely must come to you,
but this time I may not cause any woe.

If I again must rise from the dead,
I shall turn your eyes to the back of your head.

And if I again must come back from the grave,
the greatest misfortune you shall have."

Fair Ellen she walked 'cross the floor in wrath
with all her little ones in her path.

"I must go, dear children of mine;
in Heaven the angels for me pine.

25 · Just now crows the rooster so red,
back into earth must all the dead.

Just now crows the rooster so black,
– in the coppice –
Heaven's door they are closing, alack!"
– In the coppice wither the roses.

Fair Ellen walked quietly in the dark,
and all the small dogs began to bark.

The parents heard the little dogs bay,
and then they bread to the children gave.

29 • And when they heard the little dogs growl,
– in the coppice –
they lit for the children candles all.
– In the coppice wither the roses.

7 THE TALKING HARP
Recording from Zealand by H. V. Fiedler, 1847

In Odensé town there lived a man,
two beautiful daughters he had on hand.
– O Lord, O Lord, O blessed Lord!

The younger one was bright as a light,
the older one was dark as night.

Two suitors came to where they stayed,
both of them wooed the younger maid.

They both did want the younger one,
both did the older sister shun.

5 • "Now let us go to the beach and bathe
and wash ourselves so white.

Yes, wash ourselves so white
that we are both alike."
– *O Lord, O Lord, O blessed Lord!*

Ahead went the younger with flowing locks,
the older followed with evil thoughts.

The younger sat her down to bathe,
the older pushed her into the wave.

"Oh, sister dear, you save my life,
and I shall give you my silver knife."

10 · "Oh, drown, oh, drown and lose your life,
then I shall have your silver knife."

"Oh, sister dear, you see me through,
and I shall give you my bright buckled shoe."

"Oh, drown, oh, drown, pull never through,
then I shall have your bright buckled shoe."

"Oh, sister dear, you help me up,
and I shall give you my yellow locks."

"Oh, drown, oh, drown, come never up,
then I shall have your yellow locks."

15 · "Oh, sister dear, you help me on land,
and I shall give you my affianced man."

"Oh, drown, oh, drown, reach never land,
then I shall have your affianced man."

Two minstrels at the beach arrived,
and they cut off her fingers five.

And they cut off her fingers five
and made them into keys.
– *O Lord, O Lord, O blessed Lord!*

And they cut off her yellow locks
and made them into strings.

20 • "Now let's go to the town where they
are holding the big wedding today."

And first they played the strings
about the sister drowned by the bride.

And then they played once more
of the bride's sister who floated ashore.

And when they played their last,
there was the bride, into tears she burst.

On Sunday she sat on the bench of the bride,
on Monday she lay in irons tied.

25 • On Tuesday she stood in the prisoner's stand,
the next day she lay on a firebrand.
– *O Lord, O Lord, O blessed Lord!*

2 · CHRISTIANITY

8 ST. OLAV'S RACE
Svaning's Manuscript II, about 1580

King Olav and his brother
they quarreled over Norway.
– *It is so blessed to rest in Trondhjem.*

His brother
they quarreled over Norway:
He who is the best at sea,
he shall king of Norway be.

Best at sea,
he shall king of Norway be.
"How shall I succeed,
you have 'Serpent the fleet'?

Succeed,
you have 'Serpent the fleet'?"
"You take 'Serpent the fleet',
Leave 'Ox the slow' to me.

5 · The fleet,
leave 'Ox the slow' to me."
And then to church king Olav goes,
his hair like a golden halo glows.

Olav goes,
his hair like a golden halo glows.
A messenger comes for Olav to hail:
"Harold, your brother, is setting sail."

Olav to hail:
"Harold, your brother, is setting sail."
"Let them sail who want to go,
the mass we first shall listen to.
– It is so blessed to rest in Trondhjem.

Want to go,
the mass we first shall listen to.
Let them sail who want to sail,
we listen to the mass without fail.

Set sail,
we listen to the mass without fail.
Through the mass God's word we own;
my lad, break bread and set ye down.

10 · We own,
my lad, break bread and set ye down.
We'll sit down for a bite or more
and later on go to the shore.

Or more
and later on go to the shore."
They carried to the shore
both anchor and every oar.

The shore
both anchor and every oar.
King Olav walks on the sand so bleached,
the while the 'Ox' lies on the beach.

So bleached,
the while the 'Ox' lies on the beach.
He strokes the 'Ox' on the stem so white:
"Now hasten as you did last night."

So white:
"Now hasten as you did last night."
He strokes the 'Ox's side:
"Still faster you must ride."
– It is so blessed to rest in Trondhjem.

15 • 'Ox's side:
"Still faster you must ride."
"Up in the mast, my lad, you climb
and see if we'll reach Harold in time.

You climb
and see if we'll reach Harold in time."
"I see the 'Serpent' ride
away up Norway's side.

Serpent ride,
away up Norway's side."
He strokes the 'Ox's thigh:
"Go faster by and by."

'Ox's thigh:
"Go faster by and by."
The 'Ox' began to speed and shake,
the sailors couldn't stand on their legs.

And shake,
the sailors couldn't stand on their legs.
He took rope and line,
his sailors he did bind.

20 • And line,
his sailors he did bind.
And then the man at the rudder said:
"And how shall we now sail ahead?"

He said:
"And how shall we now sail ahead?"
"Sail over mountain and hillock land,
steer ahead the best you can.
– *It is so blessed to rest in Trondhjem.*

Hillock land,
steer ahead the best you can."
Then they sailed cross Skaneyarfiöll,
they all came running, every troll.

Skaneyarfiöll,
they all came running, every troll.
A hag with a spindle started to call:
"Why do you sail through my window-wall?"

To call:
"Why do you sail through my window-wall?"
Norway was Olav's prize:
at the end he led by three days.

25 • Olav's prize:
at the end he led by three days.
And on his knee the bow he bent,
the arrow into the mast it went.
– *It is so blessed to rest in Trondhjem.*

9 THE INFANT JESUS, STEPHEN AND HEROD
Erik Pontoppidan: Everriculum fermenti veteris, 1736

I shall now sharpen my pen against several prayers and songs that are remnants from the time of Papism, and I shall report some which I have happened to hear, for the benefit of my worthy collegues of the holy cloth. . . . Among them are a couple of papistic songs which I penned down according to a poor, old woman's information who sang it at my door. When I asked the woman if she believed in the truth of what she sang, she answered: God forbid that I should doubt it. Thus it was a terse conception of the blessed truth necessary to believe in. The first of the songs seems to have been picked out of a papistic book about Christ's Childhood, a dish of lies and inventions . . . The other one is of the same coinage:

An innocent maiden lived on Earth,
most beautiful ever seen;
more than all others she was worth,
they called her Heaven's queen.

Her slender neck was ermine white,
her cheeks were rosy red;
she was going to bear Our Lord,
for she was so fine a maid.

With honor Gabriel angel was sent
the Holy Virgin to see:
"I am by my Master sent,
Christ's mother you shall be."

And Mary answered and she said
what God put into her mind:
"I am the Lord his serving maid,
me shall He ready find."

5 · She carried the child for forty weeks,
did never sorrow nor mourn;
and it was on a Yulé night
that our Lord was born.

The horses St. Stephen led to the pool *NB.*
which the star helped him to find:
"Verily, now the prophet is born,
the prophet to save mankind."

And now answered King Herod aloud:
"I do not believe this thing,
unless the fried rooster does crow
on the plate and spread out his wing."

The rooster crowed and spread out his wing
at God's nativity.
Off the chair fell Herod the king
and faint and sorrow did he.

King Herod told them to bring his steed,
would ride to Bethlehem;
for there he wanted to kill the child
that aimed to fight with him. *NB.*

10 • But Mary took the child in her arms,
and Joseph bridled the ass;
and led by the Lord, through the Jewish land
toward Egypt they did pass.

11 • Some fourteen thousand tiny babes
in streams of blood he did drown;
but Jesus was ninety miles away,
before the sun went down.

10 THE SOUL OF THE CHILD

Recording from South Zealand by Franziska Carlsen, 1844

Oh, how shall the grass in the meadow thrive
– Lord Jesus forgives and brings solace –
a brother and sister they loved as man and wife.
– The Lord, my God, sent His son down to Earth.

A child they begat in sin as man and wife;
in the meadow they buried the child alive.

The child so pitifully cries,
– Lord Jesus forgives and brings solace –
its voice is heard in Paradise.
– The Lord, my God, sent His son down to Earth.

The Lord he speaks to an angel of his:
"You fetch me the child to Heaven's bliss."

5 · "Now I have come for Heaven to see,
then let me stay in eternity."

The child so pitifully cries,
its voice is heard in Paradise.

The Lord he speaks to the little child:
"Why so unhappy, why do you cry?"

"Well may I cry, well may I lament,
to Hell and its fire my mother is sent."

The Lord he speaks to an angel of his:
"You fetch me the woman to Heaven's bliss."

10 · "Both of us have come for Heaven to see,
now let us stay in eternity."

The child so pitifully cries,
its voice is heard in Paradise.

The Lord he speaks to the little child:
"Why so unhappy, why do you cry?"

"Well may I cry, well may I lament,
to Hell and its fire my father is sent."

The Lord he speaks to an angel of his:
– Lord Jesus forgives and brings solace –
"You fetch me the man to Heaven's bliss."
– The Lord, my God, sent His son down to Earth.

15 • "All three we have come for Heaven to see,
– Lord Jesus forgives and brings solace –
now let us stay in eternity."
– The Lord, my God, sent His son down to Earth.

3 · KINGS AND NOBLES

11 VALDEMAR AND TOVELIL

Ide Giöe's Manuscript, about 1630

Tovélil lives at her father's place,
two maidens they brush her hair with grace.
– Sincerely. King Valdemar loves them both dearly.

Two maidens they brush her hair with grace,
two others her locks with gold embrace.

Two others her locks with gold embrace,
two hold a mirror before her face.

Two clad her in scarlet robes with care,
two others they follow her everywhere.

5 · The king looked on and he didn't stir,
and soon he started to yearn for her.

He sent five squires to fetch her to him,
Tovélil would not follow them.

He sent nine squires as guard on her way,
Tovélil would not follow they.

The Danish king wouldn't take her No,
he let his charger for Tovélil go.

The dance was trod in the yard of the queen,
many fair maidens could there be seen.

10 · The dance was trod by two or three,
proud Tovélil was it who sang for they.
– Sincerely. King Valdemar loves them both dearly.

Eight trod the dance or nine, maybe,
proud Tovélil was it who sang for they.

The queen who at the window stood
saw Tovélil tread the silk under foot.

"Listen now, Tovélil, my dear,
lift up your train of silk so sheer."

"If I shall be queen of Denmark, I feel
I must have silk under sole and heel."

15 · "Listen now, Tovélil, my dear,
what was your morning gift, let me hear."

"He gave me the finest band of gold,
as fine as the queen did ever behold.

He gave me a chest of gold agleam,
as fine as ever in Denmark was seen.

He gave me two silver-buckled shoes,
he vowed to me to be ever true."

"Listen now, Tovélil, my friend,
how did the king get your consent?"

20 · "The king won the consent of mine,
because his power was greater than mine."

The queen she swathes her head in skin,
and then to Denmark's king she walks in.

"Listen now, Sire, lend me your ear,
why do you hold yon Tovélil so dear?"
– *Sincerely. King Valdemar loves them both dearly.*

"Why do I hold yon Tovélil so dear:
she's borne me two sons who are always near.

One is named Christof, the other Canute,
wherever I go, they follow me for good.

25 · Never do I go into a fight,
Canute and Christof are at my side."

"Be that as it may, be that as it may,
but I will have Tovélil driven away."

The queen she orders a couple of squires:
"You make the bath house as hot as a pyre.

Make the bath house as hot as a pyre,
I want yon Tovélil there to die."

The queen she orders her squires three:
"You fetch yon Tovélil here to me."

30 · Tovélil came into the hall:
"What do you want, queen, you had me called?"

"Listen now, Tovélil, my dear,
the bath house you shall for the king prepare."

In through the bath house door Tovélil trod,
the door was by the queen slammed shut.

"There's neither water nor lye about,
for Heaven's sake you let me out."

The queen she walks along Riber Street
and meets Canute and Christof, so ill at ease.
– *Sincerely. King Valdemar loves them both dearly.*

35 · "So here you are, young Christof and Canute,
go fetch your mother of the bath house out."

Christof he gave his horse the spur
and drove the steed right over her.

And when Canute this deed had seen,
he rode his steed across the queen.

Canute and Christof they said to the king:
"Now go and fetch the queen in the street."

"It doesn't matter the queen is dead,
would God let Tovélil live instead."

40 · They got Tovélil from the bath house loose,
she looked like a roasted Yuletide goose.
– *Sincerely. King Valdemar loves them both dearly.*

12 QUEEN DAGMAR'S DEATH
Svaning's Manuscript II, about 1580

Queen Dagmar lies ill in Ribé town,
in Ringsted she should have been;
all the ladies in Denmark's land
she speedily called in.
– *In Ringsted there rests Queen Dagmar.*

"Now fetch me one, now fetch me two,
now fetch me all the wise;
go and fetch me young Kirsten,
Sir Carrol's sister of Ribé."

Young Kirsten entered through the door
with honor and innocent air;
Queen Dagmar she arose once more,
so did she welcome her there.
– In Ringsted there rests Queen Dagmar.

"If you can read, if you can write
and ease my misery,
then you shall wear red velvet robes,
and you shall have my steed."

5 · "If I could read, and if I could write,
I'd do it with all my heart;
verily, in all truth I say,
your pain is very hard."

She opened the Holy Virgin's book
and read her all she could see;
verily, in all truth I say,
the tears ran down her cheeks.

They followed her out, they followed her in,
the queen sank faster and faster:
"Seeing that I won't better be,
I pray you send for my master.

Seeing that I won't better be,
I pray you send for my lord;
pray, send word to Gullandsborg,
you won't find him before."

Then her little page arose
and acted without respite;
the saddle he took off the filly grey
and saddled the steed so white.

10 • The king he stands in the castle hall
and looks so far abroad.
"Yonder I see a little page,
so sad and sorely distraught.
– In Ringsted there rests Queen Dagmar.

Yonder I see a little page,
so sadly he presses on.
God our father in Heaven knows
how it with Dagmar has gone."

Entered then the little page,
to the king he himself bestirred:
"Queen Dagmar has sent me here to you,
with you she wants a word."

The king clapped the dice board together
so that the dice they sang:
"The Lord our father in Heaven forbid
that Dagmar should die so young."

The king set out from Gullandsborg
with one hundred men, on his way;
and he rode into Ribé town
just followed by Dagmar's page.

15 • There was grief in the women's chambers,
where all the ladies cried;
Queen Dagmar she died in young Kirsten's arms
when the king into town did ride.

There was the King of Denmark,
in the doorway he did stand;
and there was young Kirsten,
she took him by the hand.

"Oh, hear ye, king of Denmark,
no more shall you grieve or mourn;
we have brought forth a son today,
from Dagmar's side he was shorn."
– In Ringsted there rests Queen Dagmar.

"I beg you, all you virgins and maids,
for God's sake hear my plea:
I beg you pray for Dagmar's soul
that she may speak to me."

With eyes as red as streaming blood
Queen Dagmar sat up in her bier:
"Alas, alas, my noble sire,
why brought you this pain to me?

20 · The first request that I beg of you,
I know you'll do it fain:
to every outlaw give him peace,
free the prisoner of his chain.

The second request that I beg of you,
it is to your boon:
do not betroth you to Bengerd,
she is a poisonous bloom.

The third request that I beg of you,
you'll grant me willingly:
pray, let Canute, my youngest son,
the king of Denmark be.

And should you not let my youngest son
Canute be Denmark's king,
Bengerd will bear another,
my son to ruin and bother.

And hadn't I last Sunday laced my sleeves
and donned my fair headdress,
then purgatory wouldn't have given me
one moment of distress.
– *In Ringsted there rests Queen Dagmar.*

25 • And hear you this, my noble sire,
if more you want me to say:
in Heaven dwell all God's angels,
they want me with them to stay."
– *In Ringsted there rests Queen Dagmar.*

13 MARSTI AND HIS WIFE
Rentzel's Manuscript, 1580–90, No. 27

Noble Marsti he went abroad,
great honor he won on his way;
Erik the king he stayed at home,
he led the wife astray.
– *The lady lingers on Zealand, so many are her sorrows.*

There was noble Marsti,
came home from feuding and war;
but his goodwife wouldn't come
to meet him as before.

Noble Marsti pondered
long with darkened face:
"Oh, why won't my beloved wife
meet me with an embrace?"

"When you left for foreign lands,
I was the spouse of a knight;
now I am queen of Denmark,
that is my shameful plight."

5 · There was the noble Marsti
reaching for his knife:
"Had I been told by somebody else,
it would have cost you your life."
– *The lady lingers on Zealand, so many are her sorrows.*

"Never more shall I go to sleep
at your side again,
ere King Erik who did me this harm
is caught by you and slain."

There was the noble Marsti
answered her not a thing;
to court he rode his charger
to stand before the king.

There was the noble Marsti,
at court he took his stand;
and he was greeted by knights and squires
and many an honest man.

Then arose King Erik
and offered him his hand:
"Welcome back, Sir Marsti,
home to country and land."

10 · Answered him Sir Marsti,
an angry man and wroth:
"I did myself the greatest harm
when I did go abroad.

I rode out of this country,
put Reval and Ri at bay,
while you have, King Erik,
led my dear wife astray."

"Harken to me, Sir Marsti,
and be not angry with me;
eight great castles on Zealand
I grant they yours shall be."
– *The lady lingers on Zealand, so many are her sorrows.*

"Harken to me, King Erik,
never in all my life
will castles eight on Zealand
be equal to my wife."

Paused Sir Marsti a long, long time,
pondering on his lot:
"I shall build a castle on Hielm,
if it cost me all I've got."

15 • Marsti rode home to his wife so fair,
a fortress on Hielm he built;
he heeded neither arrow nor gun,
nor stones from the catapult.

16 • Marsti and his wife so fair
with them did their sorrow go.
I tell you verily in truth,
it brought King Erik great woe.
– *The lady lingers on Zealand, so many are her sorrows.*

14 THE KING'S MURDER

Rentzel's Manuscript, 1580–90, No. 26; compare No. 74e

Many a man in Denmark
for royal power hopes;
and so they rode to Ribé town
and bought themselves new robes.
– *The country is in distress.*

On the night of Saint Cecilia Anno Domini MCCLXXXVI the above mentioned king Erik was slain in Finderup near Viborg.

They bought themselves new robes,
each was a cowly thing;
and then they rode into the night
to betray their rightful king.
– *The country is in distress.*

They rode into the peasant yard,
each ready with his spear;
all of them wore ashen hoods,
that none should know them there.

4 · And then they went into the barn
and gathered in their disguise.
The noble master lay awake,
he couldn't believe his eyes.

4A · [They rode their horses into the barn,
with candles did it abound;
they looked about them for the king,
whom they unhappily found.]

5 · Their spears went into his body
and through his side did they leave.
"And now we have committed the deed
o'er which all Denmark shall grieve."

5A · [It was then that Ranild
pierced the beam with his blade;
but the noble master was dead,
to him it was little aid.]

6 · When the little page-boy saw
his master suffer this fate,
he put the saddle on his steed,
no longer did he wait.

The queen she sits in the castle hall,
she looks so far and wide:
"Yonder I see the little page,
so swiftly does he ride.
– *The country is in distress.*

He's riding on my master's steed,
I fear for great disaster.
Pray our Father in Paradise,
what has become of my master?"

Entered then the little page,
and thus he did her address:
"My master is slain in the peasant's barn,
the country is in distress.

10 • My master is done to death,
may he God's mercy obtain.
Guard now the young Duke Erik
who over Denmark shall reign."

11 • "For the tidings that you have brought,
although they aren't good,
while we are alive, at the court of the king
you shall have clothing and food."
– *The country is in distress.*

15 THE BANISHMENT
Svaning's Manuscript II, about 1580

Marsti awakened at midnight:
"So strangely I have dreamt,"
spoke he to his dearest goodwife,
"may Christ know what it meant."
– *The noble master, the young Marsti.*

"I dreamt that I and my squires
across a bridge rode back;
my steed he reared and threw me off
and ran to the unbroken pack."
– *The noble master, the young Marsti.*

"Lie down, my noble master,
forget it and relax;
it means your peasants and tenants
will soon bring in the tax."

"Tomorrow the court is sitting
for the South, near the river's spring;
may God in Heaven know whom they
will blame for the death of the king."

5 · Marsti and his valiant squires
they rode to Ranisburgh,
clad in their armor, chain and swords,
they were in so great a hurry.

The queen she stands in the castle hall
and sees the advent of his band:
"Yonder comes riding Sir Marsti,
the king of the Southern land."

"Speak not, my gracious lady,
and mock me not with that name;
he is called bailiff Sir Ové
who can that title claim.

Harken, my gracious lady,
you mock me not in your hate;
he is called bailiff Sir Ové
who slept with you of late."

Answered him young King Christof,
swathed in velvet red:
"We have enough bad tidings,
now my father is dead."
– *The noble master, the young Marsti.*

10 • Answered him young King Christof
with honor and renown:
"Marsti, you shall flee from Denmark,
if I shall wear the crown."

"If I must flee from Denmark,
I shall neither shrink nor stall:
I shall fetch my food in Denmark
in summer, winter and fall."

And so he does, Sir Marsti,
when the king of exile speaks:
the isle of Hielm he fortifies
in the following two weeks.

13 • The peasant makes his way to his field,
preparing to sow his corn:
"O Lord, O Lord, pray, help us now
when the isle of Hielm has grown horn."
– *The noble master, the young Marsti.*

16 THE OUTLAWS
Svaning's Manuscript II, about 1580

There were one hundred and forty seven,
they gathered on a down:
"Where shall we go from here on,
wrathfully the king on us frown."
– *And we are driven out of Denmark.*

"We must all agree
and take what it may be."
– *But we are driven out of Denmark.*

Answered the youthful Sir Marsti:
"Sooner than that I shall fight and die.

We'll build ourselves a castle on Hielm,
we fear not the king of Denmark himself.

5 · We'll build it higher than any tower,
impregnable to all Denmark's power.

6 · So strong a castle shall here we build
to stand against guns and catapult."
– *But we are driven out of Denmark.*

17 NIELS EBBESEN
Anders Sörensen Vedel's Ballad Book, 1591

Count Gert of Holstein is slain by Sir Niels Jepsson in Randers.

After the death of King Erik Menved, his brother Christof took over the royal reign, however with varying fortune and progress; because he had, some time in the past, for the sake of his half-brother, Count Johan of Vagerland, engaged himself in open warfare with Count Gert of Holstein and some other princes who owed fealty to the count; and this long war was very harmful both to him, his children and the whole country. Neither did the good Count Gert prosper by it; he acquired a bottomless debt and lost at last his life, as told by this song. For when King Christof and his two sons had died and the country was without a king, for almost fully nine years, the native Danish noble estate did its best to chase out these harmful, foreign guests who had become too used to plunder the country and bring their booty back to Holstein. The honorable Danish hero and nobleman, Sir Niels Jepsson revolted, among others, against Count Gert, when the latter invaded Jutland, Anno Domini 1340, with eleven thousand man, and made his headquarters in Randers, almost in the middle of the country, and committed arson and rapine all around him. Sir Niels himself rode out to meet him, and when they could not reach an agreement, he defied him honestly to his face, whereafter he attacked him and slew him in Randers, on Aprilis 1., Anno Domini 1340. This Count Gert was called *Gerardus Calvus,* the Baldheaded Count, because he was somewhat bald-headed, etc.

The count he marched into Denmark's land,
him followed so great a throng;
four banners and four and twenty,
who'd dare to do him wrong?

To Randers Count Gert he wanted to go,
so had he made up his mind;
it was foretold him long ago,
he there his death would find.

But that did not deter Count Gert,
he wanted there to be;
the knights and squires, peasants and serfs
and their homes he wanted to see.

The count sent word to Niels Ebbésen
to come to Randers town;
he promised safe and peaceful road,
his word was earnest and strong.

5 • The count he met Niels Ebbésen
in the North, at Randers' shore:
"And you be welcome, Niels Ebbésen!
how fares it with you and yours?"

The count he shook Niels Ebbésen's hand,
and then they spoke for a while;
scant goodwill was seen between the two
and less of laughter and smile.

"Harken, dear Sir Niels Ebbésen,
and you be welcome here;
how are the people in North Jutland,
and what are the tidings from there?

How are your friends and your wealthy kin
and those that you hold dear?
And do you either wish to fight
or peace with me ensure?"

"People are fine in North Jutland,
each man assured and content.
Come you, Count Gert, with war or peace?
On what can we depend?

10 · For certain I have in North Jutland
both friends and wealthy kin;
and if you come with peace in mind,
their favor you shall win."

"Niels Ebbésen, you are a cunning man
and you are brave and stout;
when you can't succeed in a simple way,
you do it round about.

Then listen, Sir Niels Ebbésen,
will you join cause with me?
How many men have you here with you
that you trust with certainty?"

"I have among the Jutlanders brave
both friends and kinsmen, too;
they would right gladly follow me
and stand up to their foe.

With me I have some thirty men,
such as they well may be;
and whether fewer or more they be,
they're equally dear to me."

15 • "And if you are followed by thirty men,
your words don't match your deeds;
last night you stopped at Sir Buggé's castle
with one hundred armored steeds."

Sharply Niels Ebbésen answered him
as he took one step back:
"And whether he is a knight or squire
who told you a lie so black;

and whether it is a man or a woman
who dares to tell that lie,
I'll never yield him a foot of ground,
and he or I must die."

"Harken, dear Sir Niels Ebbésen,
forget it, 'tween me and you,
and ride to your friend Sir Buggé and ask,
if he'll to me be true."

"And shall I ride on your errand away
and to Sir Buggé go,
what shall I tell him on your behalf?
You first must let me know."

20 · "Already Sir Buggé has challenged me,
young Powel Glob, he, too;
Sir Anders Frost is another one,
a leader of your crew.

And you yourself, Niels Ebbésen,
have squires eating your bread
who erstwhile in my service were,
till from my house they fled.

The first is youthful Eské Frost
and also his brothers two;
without my Yes and without my leave
from my service they withdrew.

Still others have I tried to please,
to thwart me now they dare;
and if you take Sir Buggé's counsel,
you'll see how you shall fare."

"Sir Buggé's counsel I do not know
or what he intends to do;
but a true servant was Anders Frost,
that none knows better than you.

25 · Sir Anders Frost is an able man,
himself he can defend;
and did he wish his leave to take,
how could you refuse consent?

It always was custom in Denmark's land,
useless for you to grieve:
whoever will not stay in service,
then he may take his leave.

Nobody's ever married together
but for the monk and his hood:
squire rides and squire stays
where he finds the service good."

Answered him then the count Sir Gert,
roused by what he heard him say:
"No one may take leave of his master,
who wants that he shall stay.

Harken to me, Niels Ebbésen,
too long you have harangued;
either you shall from Denmark flee,
or I shall have you hanged.

30 · Peacefully up to me you rode,
now peacefully go from me;
if I had not pledged my word,
a different end you'd see."

"You gave me your knightly word of peace,
as long as you will allow;
harken, Count Gert, if you mean me harm,
you'll rue it well enow.

Thieves you may on the gallows hang
for ravens and eagles wild;
you cannot easily make me flee
from Denmark, from wife and child.

If I should flee from my fatherland
and from my children and wife,
scornfully you would surely speak
of me the rest of your life."

"Be on your way, Niels Ebbésen,
I do not want to hear you;
else I shall break my armor on you,
so very little I fear you."

35 · "Nobody ever saw me so scared
that I did not dare to quake.
Harken, Sir Gert, keep this in mind,
watch out for your very own sake."

"You talk so much about hurting me,
Niels Ebbésen, as you think best:
until tomorrow you've peace from me,
until the sun goes to rest.

This day and also the next till eve
are yours, that is all you have left;
were I not a true count's son,
I soon shall be your guest."

"Count Gert, you are a fiery man,
a knight both brave and stout;
when you can't win the day by force,
you try it round about."

Away rode Sir Niels Ebbésen
the while he waved his hand:
"Remember, Count Gert, I soon again
shall here before you stand."

40 · Niels Ebbésen hastened down the road,
his horse he lightly spurred.
Behind stood the count and all his men,
to chase him nobody dared.

He rode away with greatest speed
and at his house he arrived;
he told his tale to his lovely wife
and asked her for advice.

"I hail you, dearest wife of mine,
your best advice you say:
the count will drive me out of the land,
he threatened me yesterday.

Two choices he gave me, both were grim,
the third was neither a joke:
I must swear to him or flee the land
or be hanged on the gallows, he spoke."

"What counsel comes to my mind to give,
I'm but a modest wife:
the worst advice may be the best,
if you can bring it to life.

45 · The worst advice may be the best
if you can bring it to life:
either you burn him in his hall
or put him to the knife.

Then have your steeds to the smithy sent,
new shoes for all the nags;
have all the shoes put backwards on
that none shall know your tracks.

Have all the shoes put backwards on,
your tracks they'll know them not;
and never tell a living soul
you were by a woman taught."

"Eat and drink, my stalwart lads,
be merry and do not frown;
for when the night has come to an end,
we'll meet the dawn in town.

Ere the sun goes up for another day,
news we shall hear and see;
for every man, to his master true,
must not from his master flee."

50 · Then arose all the squires bold,
they pledged themselves anew,
but for Niels Ebbésen's sister's son,
only he wished to flee.

The squires swore a solemn oath
that they would venture their life
and follow him ever courageously
when he would wage a strife.

And so they rode to Fruerlund,
there each one tied his steed;
then they went into Randers town,
the bald-headed count to see.

There was Sir Niels Ebbésen,
when Randers' bridge he saw:
"Any man who won't follow me
may take his leave right now."

Forward strode yon little Svend Tröst,
most trusted of all his force:
"My master, give me leave right now,
and also saddle and horse."

55 • He asked for leave and was granted it
and also saddle and steed;
that very day, before evening came,
he served his master in need.

Sir Niels Ebbésen rode to the door,
a plan he had in mind:
with sharpened sword he struck the door
which the count hovered behind.

"Master, arise from your sleep at once
and open the door, pray do;
your dear brother, Count Henrik,
he has sent me to you."

"Though you be sent by brother mine,
still your request is wrong:
meet me tomorrow in the church
'tween mass and evensong."

"Then let your page come to the door
to take this letter of his;
for Ribé lies dangerously besieged,
and Kolding in ashes is.

60 • Ribé lies dangerously besieged,
aflame are Vejlé and Kolding;
verily, Niels Ebbésen's bones
on the gibbet are molding."

"And is it true what you tell me now,
then are the tidings good:
you shall be treated with honor and care
while we are living both.

Now open up and don't delay
and let the messenger in:
victory is won, the country is quelled,
these are the tidings he brings."

Then through the window the count looked out,
saw many a shiny spear:
"So haplessly I to Denmark came,
Niels Ebbésen is out there!"

They struck the door with their shields and spears,
broke every spike and post.
"If you are in, you bald-headed count,
then we shall drink your toast!"

65 · "Oh, take a seat, Niels Ebbésen,
and better we will get on;
now we shall send for Henrik the Duke,
also Claus Krumdige, my son."

"Yesterday you sang another tune
when out at Randers' strand:
either you wanted to have me hanged,
or I should flee the land."

Up, then, stood the count's little page,
he was of Niels Ebbésen's clan:
"If you are fooled by honeyed words,
we'll be ruined, every man."

And then spoke the dirt-black squire,
he wasn't clean nor white:
"Now put an end to the many words,
and let the sword blades bite."

"I haven't mansions or castles strong
can keep a prisoner so rich;
so do not spare the whetted swords
and let them fiercefully swish."

70 • And then they took hold of the yellow locks
of the rugged madman's head
and sliced his neck with one fell sweep
against the post of the bed.

And when the count was done to death,
with drums they called the men;
to leave the town as the deed was done,
ordered Niels Ebbésen.

He hurried his men out of town,
he dared no longer stay;
there he was met by Sir Ové Hals
who wanted to bar his way.

"O harken to me, Sir Ové Hals,
my brother-in-law so true,
you mustn't do me any harm,
but you must let me through."

"Full well I know our family ties,
as close as they can be:
but you have stabbed my master to death,
I shall not let you flee."

75 • The sheep they bleat, the geese they hiss,
the cocks crow on the walls;
Sir Ové Hals was in a plight,
for help by the Holsteins he calls.

The Danes he could no longer resist,
for the Holsteins he had to call;
the count was killed at daylight
and not in the night at all.

And then they bared their valiant swords,
Niels Ebbésen wouldn't give in;
he cut the head off Sir Ové Hals,
in no other way could he win.

Niels Ebbésen came to Randers' bridge,
and there was gore and grief;
and there he found yon little Svend Tröst
who erst had taken leave.

Niels Ebbésen rides across Randers' bridge,
the Holsteins after him ride;
but little Svend Tröst he stayed behind,
alone the bridge he destroyed.

80 · Praise to Niels Ebbésen's sister's son,
to his uncle so true a man:
the timber fell into the bay so fast,
the Holsteins found no span.

Niels Ebbésen came to the house of a crone,
where only two loaves could be found;
but one she gave to Niels Ebbésen,
he killed the bald-headed count.

God save thy soul, Niels Ebbésen,
a Danish hero thou art:
so gladly you saw the foreign guests
from your fatherland depart.

83 • Christ's blessing on every Danish lad
who both with tongue and with hand
with loyal zeal, without sham or deceit
will save his fatherland.

18 THE EAGLE SONG (CHRISTIAN II)
Anna Basse's Manuscript, before 1616

All the small birds that live in the wood
the hawk they clamor about;
he tears off their backs both feathers and down,
from the wood he'll drive them out.
– But the eagle builds in the rockies afar.

They gather them for a council anew
in the top of an old oak tree;
how to find a king for themselves,
from the hawk to set them free.

Up then stood the crow so poor,
so full of worry and care:
"Let us choose the old eagle,
I hope he will be fair."

Right away the other small birds
said yes and agreed upon 't:
"Now is the eagle king of the birds
as long as God may want."

5 • Answered them the hawk so proud:
"We won't allow it at all;
for if the eagle be king of the birds,
he'll reign to our downfall."

When the old eagle heard of this,
it made him angry and cross;
then he struck the hawk so proud,
hard with his piercing claws.
– *But the eagle builds in the rockies afar.*

And this gladdens the other small birds,
each sings his very best;
joyous warbling fills the wood,
where the eagle builds his nest.

Together came the host of hawks,
they covered both forest and lake:
"We will fly to the bosket
and war we there shall make."

This was heard by the lowly dove,
she flew to the eagle and said:
"The host of hawks is now on the way,
to do you harm they threat'."

10 · Then the grey eagle answered her
with tears in his eyes to see:
"So many mice can bite a cat,
I must from the bosket flee."

Away then flew the eagle grey
together with his brood;
the little birds flew here and there,
they knew not what to do.

The hawks sit now in the oak tree top,
with outspread wings they rest;
the other small birds in the bosket dwell
woefully and suppressed.

The crow now hungers on naked twig,
sits cringing on her claw;
the owl she hides in the bramble bush,
I think, in fear and awe.
– *But the eagle builds in the rockies afar.*

The peewit runs in the ditch between fields,
she flees, but shows her top;
the hawk he now comes swooping down,
he takes and eats her up.

15 · And all the other small birds sit
as silent and still as stone;
now they have lost their beautiful song,
if God wills, they'll sing anon.

Now there is sorrow in the wood
the birds once filled with song;
the poor little birds, I pity them,
for them time seems so long.

The dog lies under the table and sleeps,
the fox is among the geese;
but when God wills, he'll waken again
for his poor geese to free.

The cat is ill and lies in the yard,
hated by everyone;
the mouse reigns e'en in the beggar's bag
and makes him woebegone.

19 · May God then help the poor old eagle
who flies 'cross the heath so dreary;
he finds himself neither place nor shelter
where he can build his eyrie.
– *But the eagle builds in the rockies afar.*

19 FREDERIK II IN THE DITMARSH

Recorded near Copenhagen by J. N. Vinther, about 1875

King Fredrik he rides to Ditmarsh land
with face so merry and hat so grand.
– *The Ditmarsh masters they've lost their fields and fallows.*

He stayed for days and he stayed for four
and seized both bulwarks and walls and more.

He stayed for days and he stayed for ten
and seized both towns and castles in them.

The Ditmarsh masters prepare a feast,
King Fredrik himself partakes in it.

5 · King Fredrik he uses fork and knife
on which his own name is inscribed.

The Ditmarsh masters together planned
how Fredrik might fall into their hands.

But late at night when the dew did fall
a maiden went out on Fredrik to call.

She came to his door and there she knocked:
"Arise, King Fredrik, remove the lock."

"King Fredrik of Denmark we never were,
but only a merchant, as you have heard."

10 · "Of course, thou art Fredrik, the Danish king,
and thou wilt be caught this very evening."

King Fredrik jumped out of his bed so fast,
he drew the bolts both in and out.

"Listen, my maid, thou be true to me,
ten barrels of gold I shall give to thee.

Thou saddle my charger, but hurry, do;
I'll tie my clothes 'round my charger's shoe."
– The Ditmarsh masters they've lost their fields and fallows.

King Fredrik he rode to the ferryman:
"Thou take me across the bay right now."

15 • "I'd willingly do it, but I don't dare,
for this both master and council forbid."

"I give thee thalers, I give thee five,
thou take me across the bay alive."

"I'd willingly do it, but I don't dare,
for this both master and council forbid."

"I give thee five thalers, I give thee ten,
thou take me across the bay for them."

"I'd willingly do it, but I don't dare,
for this both master and council forbid."

20 • King Fredrik he draws his sword so blue,
the ferryman he runs through and through.

The gloves off his hands King Fredrik draws
and starts himself to use the oars.

And when King Fredrik had rowed some more
he saw the Ditmarsh masters on shore.

King Fredrik he doffs his hat so light
and bade the Ditmarsh masters good night.

"If thou wert of noble blood, my maid,
gladly, I swear, I would have thee wed.

25 • But I shall give thee another good man,
also an earldom in my land."
– The Ditmarsh masters they've lost their fields and fallows.

4 · SAGA AND MYTH

20 SVEND NORMAND ("SVEND VONVED")
Langebek's Folio Manuscript, about 1630

One evening, at the ingle fire,
Svend Normand played his golden lyre.
– *Look around you, Svend Normand.*

He played the lyre in secrecy,
his mother came walking in, did she.

"Better if you would ride
among the warriors and fight –

Avenging the death of your sire
than playing my golden lyre."

5 · Svend Normand fastens his sword at his side
as if he were riding out to fight.

"When shall I be ready with the brew,
when shall I once more be seeing you?"

"When stones begin to float
and ravens are getting white."

"Never the stones shall float,
and never the ravens get white."

"Never the stones shall float,
you shall never expect me home."

10 · "Well, then I shall foretell:
your journey will not end well.
– *Look around you, Svend Normand.*

So be it fateful for you abroad
and fateful for your valiant sword."

He stroked her cheek: "O mother dear,
be quiet now and never fear."

"Then I shall cast a spell:
fare well abroad, fare well.

With victory in your horse's foot
and victory in your sword so good."

15 · On mountain paths he looked around,
the strangest warriors he found.

He looked behind, the lynx was there,
and on his right he had a bear.

"Now harken, warrior, mindfully,
you shall trade animals with me."

"Nobody's challenge I ever knew,
since the time I King Carol slew."

Svend Normand listened and laughed with glee:
"My father's slayer you then must be."

20 · They fought all day and the following day,
and on the third they were still at the fray.

But on the fourth day, at twilight
Svend Normand killed the evil knight.

Svend Normand fastened the sword at his side
and farther abroad he wanted to ride.
– *Look around you, Svend Normand.*

And he came to a moorland house,
there was a shepherd tending cows.

"Harken, shepherd, and tell me true:
who owns the herd that's tended by you?

25 · What is rounder than the wheel?
Where does one drink the merriest yule?"

"The sun is rounder than the wheel,
in heaven they have the merriest yule."

"And what fills every dell?
At parties, who dresses well?"

"The snow fills every dell,
at parties, man dresses well."

"What's blacker than the sloe?
What's noisier than the drum?"

30 · "Sin's blacker than the sloe,
Thunder noisier than the drum."

"What is the broadest span?
Who is most loathsome to man?"

"The ice is the broadest span,
the troll is most loathsome to man."

"Where is the highest road?
Where is the basest drink?"

"In Heaven's the highest road,
in Hell the basest drink."
– *Look around you, Svend Normand.*

35 • "Where do you find house and cheer
with room for warriors there?"

"Yonder are house and cheer,
and warriors use to stay there."

He took a gold ring off his fist
and placed it on the shepherd's wrist.

"You are the only man on Earth
who got of Svend Normand a thing of worth."

Sven Norman fastened the sword at his side,
home to his mother he wanted to ride.

40 • When he came to the castle gate,
fifteen witches sat there in state.

Out of the sheath the sword he drew,
and all the fifteen witches he slew.

42 • His mother's fate was just as grim,
she was also cut down by him.
– *Look around you, Svend Normand.*

21 ANGELFYR AND HELMER KAMP
Anna Basse's Manuscript, before 1616, see No. 74 d

Ové lives at Udés-ker,
rich in friends and gold;
he has also two fine sons,
he knows they're brave and bold.
– *The North wind blows the rain across the beaches.*

And it was young Helmer Kamp,
to Opsal he wanted to ride;
he ordered them to saddle his horse:
"I'll ask the princess for my bride."
– *The North wind blows the rain across the beaches.*

Answered him young Angelfyr,
dressed in velvet red:
"Hark, this evening you shall not
win the beautiful maid."

Ordered then young Angelfyr:
"Hark and saddle my steed;
I shall ride to Opsal today,
the earth'll crack under his feet."

5 · When they came to the castle yard,
they dressed in fur and skin,
then they went into the hall
and stood before the king.

Entered first young Helmer Kamp,
before the throne he stood:
"Sire, give me that daughter of yours,
give me your answer good."

Entered then young Angelfyr
with gold rings on his hand:
"Sire, give me that daughter of yours
and hie yourself off your land."

Long stood the king of Opsal
and thought what he should do;
long he wondered what he should
answer the warriors two.

Then the king of Opsal
at last he did respond:
"I'll give my daughter to the man
that she herself will want."
– The North wind blows the rain across the beaches.

10 • "Thank you, thanks, my father dear,
you leave it up to me:
Give me to young Helmer Kamp,
he shall my husband be.

I will not have young Angelfyr,
for he is halfway a troll:
so is his father, so is his mother,
so are his kinsmen all."

There was then young Angelfyr
he answered her and said:
"Let us go into the yard
and fight about the maid."

'Twas the king of Opsal
who spoke what he had to say:
"The lads are strong, the swords are sharp,
then let them do it that way."

And there was young Angelfyr
he drew his sword from his belt,
and there was young Helmer Kamp
whom by the sword he felled.

15 • Back at Udés-ker Ové stands,
looking far away:
"I wonder what's happened to Helmer,
my heart is filled with dismay."

Back at Udés-ker Ové stands,
looking across the heath:
"What was it that irked my sons today,
why were they in such a wrath?"
– *The North wind blows the rain across the beaches.*

And Ové jumped on his charger,
so furiously did he ride
that he arrived at the Opsal king's,
just before Helmer died.

"Harken, dear son, young Helmer Kamp,
I do not understand,
how it was that your valiant sword
was wavering in your hand."

"I have got eight fatal wounds,
so deeply I am stung:
even with only one of them
I couldn't have lasted long."

20 · There was Ové from Udés-ker
he drew his sword from his belt;
and there was young Angelfyr
whom by the sword he felled.

"Just you lie, young Angelfyr,
and bleed to death for your deed;
it hurt my heart a thousandfold
when I saw Helmer bleed.

22 · Just you lie, young Angelfyr,
and die without recall;
it hurt my heart a thousandfold
when I saw Helmer fall."
– *The North wind blows the rain across the beaches.*

22 HAVBOR AND SIGNE
Langebek's Folio Manuscript, about 1630

Havbor the king and Sivord the king
quarreled till one was dead
about the young proud Signélil,
she was a lovely maid.
– *You'll never win one that lovely.*

Havbor awoke at midnight,
about his dreams he spake;
his mother listened intently to him,
as she was lying awake.

"I dreamt I was in Denmark,
to Aasebro I came;
I had a candle of wax in my hand,
then died the burning flame."

"The vivid dreams that you have dreamt,
a lovely maid did cause;
and now I shall send for somebody
who can explain them to us."

5 · Havbor and his mother
they stayed at home, the two,
and so they send for a woman
who could the dreams construe.

There was the soothsayer woman,
stood under the castle beam;
then Havbor, son of the king, arose
and told her of his dream:

"Your fortune has determined
you'll win the maid for your bride;
but you take care, young Havbor,
you do not pay with your life."

Havbor lets his hair grow long,
and women's clothes they sew;
then he rode to Denmark,
so many to sorrow and rue.
– *You'll never win one that lovely.*

There was Havbor, son of the king,
dressed in velvet all;
to meet proud Signélil face to face
he went into the hall.

10 · "So here you are, proud Signélil,
so well attended to;
Havbor has sent me here to you
that you should teach me to sew."

"With all the needlework I know
I'll gladly give you aid;
you shall sit at table with me
and sleep at night with my maid."

"With royal children I have dined,
been sleeping at their side;
if tonight I sleep with your maid,
I'll die in this great plight.

Harken to me, lovely maid,
and do not further fret;
you shall sit at table with me
and later sleep in my bed."

And all the lovely maidens sat
and sewed as they knew best;
Havbor, son of the king, the needle
between his lips had pressed.

15 • And all the lovely maidens sat
and talked as they were able,
while the youthful Havbor
drew animals on the table.
– *You'll never win one that lovely.*

He drew the stag, he drew the doe
as they ran through the wood;
proud Signélil copied his animals
and sewed the best she could.

The serving woman noticed it
while walking to and fro:
"I never saw a maiden who
less able was to sew.

Never she sews the smallest seam,
the needle in mouth she has;
never so great a goblet was found,
that too big for her it was."

"Harken to me, my serving maid,
you stop your mockery;
whether you choose to go in or out,
it's all the same to me."

20 • And when the day was growing old
and it was almost night,
proud Signélil she bade her maids
two waxen candles to light.

They lit the waxen candles,
so nicely they were made,
and escorted young Havbor
up to proud Signélil's bed.

"Now we are alone, please, tell me,
lovely Signélil mine,
is there nobody in the world
for whom your heart does pine?"
– *You'll never win one that lovely.*

"Nobody know I in the world
for whom my heart does pine,
excepting Havbor, son of the king,
and he may not be mine."

"If it is Havbor, son of the king,
the one that you hold dear,
then you shall know, proud Signélil,
with you he rests so near."

25 · "Harken, Havbor, son of the king,
why bring me this disgrace?
Why didn't you ride to my father's house
and ask him face to face?"

Answered her Havbor, son of the king,
with truth and modesty:
"Your father is a hot-tempered man,
he wouldn't answer me."

"Harken, Havbor, son of the king,
there may be woe and strife,
if my father hear about this,
it surely will cost you your life."

"I have a sword, the very best,
'tis lying at my head;
and were there thirty stalwart men,
I wouldn't be afraid.

And at my feet is lying
an armor made for me;
and were there thirty well armed men,
I would never flee."
– *You'll never win one that lovely.*

30 • Havbor, son of the king, knew not
they were alone no more;
outside stood the serving maid
and listened at the door.

She robbed him of his valiant sword
and of his armor ring,
and back into the hall she went,
showed it to Sivord, the king.

"Awake, awake, King Sivord,"
– his eyes were closed so tight –
"young Havbor, son of the king, is sleeping
with your daughter tonight."

Sivord, the king of Denmark,
he shouted through the hall:
"Arise, my men, and arm yourselves,
hurry, one and all.

Arise, my men, rise, one and all,
let nothing be amiss;
for it is Havbor, son of the king,
a stubborn fighter he is."

35 • And they pounded on the door
with sword and with baselard:
"Awake, awake, young Havbor,
and come into the yard."

His hand groped on the pillow,
his sword it wasn't there.
"Arise, proud Signélil, arise,
this seems to me so queer.
– *You'll never win one that lovely.*

Harken, my proud Signélil,
of your love I must have proof:
when you see that I am dead,
set fire to your roof."

Praise to Havbor, son of the king,
he fought them stroke for stroke;
they couldn't overcome him
before the bedpost broke.

They tied his hands so firmly
with ropes that they laid on:
there was Havbor, son of the king,
he broke everyone.

40 · But the serving maid came in
and spoke as she saw fit:
"Take a hair of Signélil's
and bind his hands with it.

If a hair of Signélil's
into a chain you make,
with the love he has for her,
this he will never break."

They laid a hair of Signélil's
on his hands and tied him:
that he had no heart to break,
and never he defied them.

They took Havbor, son of the king,
into the countryside
and hanged him on the gallows tree;
men sorrowed far and wide.
– *You'll never win one that lovely.*

But before, young Havbor said,
so sorrowful was he:
"Take my cloak and hang it first,
that I would like to see.

45 • Take my cloak and hang it first,
that I would like to see
and whether my proud Signélil
then glad or sad will be."

With dignity and firmness
proud Signélil she cries:
"Then I shall kill myself today,
join Havbor in Paradise.

Many around the king are glad
for Havbor's death, I fear;
but now I shall seek vengeance
on those whom they hold dear."

She set fire to her dwelling,
all in its width and breadth;
under her silken bolster
Signélil choked to death.

The news were spread by the little page,
dressed with taste and grace:
"Signélil and her lovely maids
are burning in her place."

50 · "Hand me down my mantle
and fling it on the earth;
if I had one thousand lives,
none would be anything worth."
– *You'll never win one that lovely.*

"Some run down to Signélil,
for burnt she mustn't be;
and others don't let Havbor
die on the gallows tree."

But on the gallows Havbor
into a corpse had turned;
and in her dwelling Signélil
was already burnt.

"If I'd known beforehand
their love was so deep and grand,
I wouldn't have done this deed today
for all of Denmark's land."

54 · Havbor they hanged and Signélil burnt,
they did of their lives deprive;
and the accurséd serving maid
they buried her alive.
– *You'll never win one that lovely.*

23 SVEND FELDING
Karen Brahe's Folio Manuscript, about 1583

There was Sir Svend Felding
one day he rode to Rome;
all Danish pilgrims had to praise
that once he there did come.

There was Sir Svend Felding
from Denmark ready to ride,
he called upon a proud maiden
so late an eventide.

He called upon a lady proud,
a lady like none about;
she placed him uppermost at the table,
o'er all the knightly crowd.

She placed him uppermost at the table,
o'er all the knightly crowd;
and then she asked Svend Felding himself,
whence he had ridden out.

5 • She looked then at his shirt,
embroidered with gold of the best:
"This cannot be a pilgrim
we have tonight as guest.

This cannot be a pilgrim
we have tonight as guest;
'tis either the king of Denmark
or one of the very best."

"I am not king of Denmark,
my state is not so grand;
I am but a poor pilgrim,
born in Denmark's land.

Harken to me, proud maiden,
angry you mustn't be;
many a child in Denmark is born,
each to his destiny."

"But I have heard throughout the years
that Danish men are so bold;
I praise and thank our Father in Heaven
that one I now behold.

10 · If you will hear me, noble knight,
I'll tell my woe to you:
we have an evil ogre here,
he'll ruin my land all through.

We have an evil ogre here,
he'll ruin my lands for good;
he doesn't want any other fare
than maidens and ladies as food."

"If I had horse, and I had harness
that suited all my needs,
then I would do it for your sake
and break with the ogre a spear."

Then they led out the Spanish steeds,
white as a white-washed wall;
Svend Felding laid his hand on their head,
like curs to earth did they fall.

"Now I would pay with gold so red
one hundred marks or more,
if I had just a Danish horse,
in Denmark bred and born."

15 · Then forward came a miller-man,
his words went far and wide:
"I have a goodly Danish mare
for him who dares to ride.

At home I have a Danish mare,
is born in Sæbylund,
and every time she comes to the mill
she carries a thousand pounds."

"Listen, my friendly miller-man,
your horse just let me see;
then surely shall we Danish two
fight against Romans three."

And when the horse was brought in sight,
it was as the miller said;
the hoof was high, the chest was broad,
Sven Felding saddled the steed.

He saddles the horse so tight, so tight,
as tightly as he pleases;
the horse sinks down right to her knees,
the strap goes all to pieces.

20 • "Some fifteen rings of gold so good
with me from Denmark I brought;
if I now had a saddle strap
it should with them be bought."

There were the ladies and maidens so proud,
a saddle strap they made:
quarter-thick and two feet wide,
they to Svend Felding gave.

Svend Felding took off his gloves so small,
his hands were soft and white;
himself he strapped the valiant horse,
he dared not his squire abide.

He strapped the horse so tight, so tight,
it fitted his needs and mood;
again the horse before him knelt,
Svend Felding now understood.

"And had I known, my valiant horse,
that you had sense like a man,
I would have loosened the strap a notch,
before I mounted your back."

25 · When first they jousted, when first they clashed,
none of the fighters would yield;
Svend Felding his spear was broke in two,
his shield flew into the field.

Svend Felding thought of so good a plan,
himself of best avail:
"You meet me tomorrow in the field,
I'll be there without fail."

He hurried to the chapel
and had the last rites there;
the holy wafer he carried away
and put on the shaft of his spear.

"Now take away the crowned spear,
for I can use it for naught;
and bring to me a schooner mast,
with better I never fought."

And when they jousted, and when they clashed,
both fighters were full of wrath;
the evil ogre he broke his neck,
his head flew into the heath.

30 • His head in five, his back in nine,
his legs in pieces most;
Svend Felding rode up to the lovely maid
to greet her and pledge a toast.

And she sent out nine knights so bold
to lift him off his filly:
"Land and country we'll give to you,
if you will marry the lily."

"No, for I have a maiden betrothed,
a master's daughter of Rome;
if I fail to be true to her,
I shall never be condoned.

For I have a maiden betrothed
in the Eastern King's domain;
for seven barrels of gold so red
her I would never forsake.

So let instead a town be built,
the very best you can;
and promise that shelter you always will give
to pilgrims who come to this land.

35 • When Danish pilgrims come hither,
spare neither wine nor bread;
pray heartily for Svend Felding,
already for ages dead."

5 · LOVE AND DEATH

24 NILUS AND HILLELIL
Svaning's Manuscript I, about 1580

There was brave Sir Nilus
from home he rode away;
he betrothed proud Hillélil,
she was so fair a maid.
– *They act out a play, and the play was nothing but anger.*

They drank at the wedding
every day through five;
on the sixth at evening
they followed home the bride.

They had horses saddled,
away her wain they haled;
when they come to the moorland
there blows so strong a gale.

"It rains and it is windy
and cold and won't relent;
tell me, my proud Hillélil,
where to unfold our tent.

5 · If we ride to Hörringsholm,
it is so long a path;
if we ride to Fredélund,
your uncle harbors me wrath."

"Let us ride to Fredélund
and rest ourselves tonight,
and be my mother's brother there,
your peace I shall make right."
– *They act out a play, and the play was nothing but anger.*

There was brave Sir Nilus
into the yard rode in;
and there stood Sir Peter,
swathed in fur and skin.

"Here you are, Sir Peter,
you are my uncle dear;
give Sir Nilus roof tonight
for him and all his men."

"God be with you, proud Hillélil,
you did no fortune find;
a man that was far richer
for you I had in mind."

10 • "A man that was far richer
for me you had in mind;
but none I could love better
you any place would find."

"I will give him roof tonight
for him and those he binds;
but well he knows, Sir Nilus,
he slew a brother of mine."

They followed then proud Hillélil
to her chamber for to sleep;
they followed then brave Sir Nilus
into the banquet hall.

Poured they for brave Sir Nilus
both mead and wine again;
out he goes, Sir Peter,
arms himself and his men.
– *They act out a play, and the play was nothing but anger.*

Entered then Sir Peter,
his sword on the table he threw:
"Did you forget, Sir Nilus,
my brother was slain by you?"

15 · "No, full well I know it,
as if it were yesterday;
I'll be a brother to you,
as long as live I may."

"You and all your squires,
my peace you need not fear;
but your sister's two sons they shall
stay and serve me here."

Up then rose the warriors two
with swords girt at their waist:
"My master, give us now your leave,
and we will solve our fate."

There stood brave Sir Nilus
looking at the affray,
until both his sister's sons
dead on the flooring lay.

"I promised once by the holy grave
the Lord did suffer in death,
I never would draw my sword on a Sunday
except in sore distress."

20 • Up stood brave Sir Nilus
and drew his sword from his sash;
verily, I tell you,
valiantly did he slash.
– *They act out a play, and the play was nothing but anger.*

There was brave Sir Nilus
he slashed with might and main
so long, until his valiant sword
wore out and broke in twain.

He shielded himself with cushions
and bolsters high and low;
outside the door of the banquet hall
he got the fatal blow.

Then said brave Sir Nilus
with sorrow and with woe:
"Be ready now, proud Hillélil,
for it is time to go."

There was brave Sir Nilus
mounted his horse so white,
and then he rode to Hermindsholm,
he rode the best he might.

25 • There was brave Sir Nilus
into the yard rode in;
there stood his dear sister,
swathed in fur and skin.

"Welcome to you, dear brother,
why do alone you ride?
Where may my two sons be
who should be at your side?"

"I rode on to Fredélund,
Hillélil counseled so;
and there your two sons now remain,
I got the fatal blow.
– *They act out a play, and the play was nothing but anger.*

Listen, my dear sister,
now make a bed for me,
and be to proud Hillélil a mother,
the fairest woman is she."

"How can I to Hillélil
be a mother good?
By her I lost two sons of mine
and my brother in his own blood."

30 · There was woe in the chambers
and there was still more harm;
there was brave Sir Nilus
died in his sister's arm.

31 · There died brave Sir Nilus,
there was great sorrow and fear;
proud Hillélil laid her in his arms
and died with him she held dear.
– *They act out a play, and the play was nothing but anger.*

25 EBBE SKAMMELSEN
Sofia Sandberg's Manuscript, before 1622

Skammel he lives up here in Thy,
merry and well to do;
he has five sons so proud and strong,
two of them came to woe.
– *And thus roams Ebbé Skammelsen on many stormy trails.*

Three of them died long ago,
the other two were left;
verily, I tell you,
they were brave and deft.
– *And thus roams Ebbé Skammelsen on many stormy trails.*

Ebbé was the younger,
he rode far and wide;
proud Adéluds, the lovely maid,
he asked to be his bride.

Proud Adéluds, the lovely maid,
he asked her for her troth;
then he took her home to his mother,
and then he rode abroad.

5 • Ebbé serves in the house of the king
and acts with honor there;
Peter, his brother, stays at home
and courts the maid he has dear.

There was Peter Skammelsen
he dressed in velvet all,
looking for proud Adéluds
he went into the hall.

"Here I find you, proud Adéluds,
give me your troth and grace;
I shall honor and love you
all my living days."

"Be silent, Peter Skammelsen,
don't talk this way to me;
I'm betrothed to your brother,
this shall never be."

Answered Peter Skammelsen,
richly in velvet dressed:
"Ebbé serves in the house of the king,
to him you are just a jest."
– *And thus roams Ebbé Skammelsen on many stormy trails.*

10 · Then said Ebbé's mother,
for him she didn't care:
"You take Peter Skammelsen,
Ebbé is false, I swear.

Ebbé serves in the house of the king
and acts with honor there;
a maiden in the house of the queen
he yearns for and holds dear.

Better you take my older son,
with castles golden-red,
than wait for Ebbé Skammelsen,
he loves another maid."

"Harken, Peter Skammelsen,
you take another wife;
no other man shall bind me
while Ebbé is still alive."

Answered her Ebbé's mother,
her voice had an honest ring:
"I'll tell you the truth, proud Adéluds,
Ebbé he died last spring."

15 · Then proud Adéluds stood up,
the delightful rose,
and she gave Peter Skammelsen
her silken hand in troth.

They prepared for the wedding
and bought both wine and brew;
Ebbé served in the house of the king,
so little about it he knew.
– And thus roams Ebbé Skammelsen on many stormy trails.

Ebbé awoke at midnight
and told what he had dreamt;
his companion lay awake
thinking of what it meant.

"I thought I saw my stone house
in flames and all alight;
there burned my brother Peter
together with my bride."

"You thought you saw your stone house
in flames and all alight:
that is because your brother
betrothed your lovely bride."

20 • Then arose young Ebbé
and tied the sword at his side,
then he asked for furlough,
as homeward he would ride.

There was Ebbé Skammelsen
he rode a furious race,
three days he used to ride the road
that erst took thirty days.

There was Ebbé Skammelsen
he rode so fast away,
he came to his father's house
on the first wedding day.

There was Ebbé Skammelsen
rode into his father's yard;
there he saw a little page,
dressed in a mantle smart.
– *And thus roams Ebbé Skammelsen on many stormy trails.*

"Harken to me, my little page,
and answer me my query:
who are all these people here
who're gathered and make merry?"

25 · "All these people that you see
who are gathered here,
came as Peter, your brother
weds the maid you have dear."

Entered then his sisters two
and welcomed with joy their brother;
they were gladder to see him again
than both his father and mother.

To one he gave a diadem,
the other a golden band,
both he had bought for his lovely bride,
brought from a foreign land.

[To one he gave a golden band,
the other a gold ring so wide;
both he had brought from a foreign land,
brought for his lovely bride.]

Ebbé he turned his steed around,
he wanted to ride away;
but his mother took hold of the reins,
demanding that he should stay.

30 · Doggedly she held on to the reins,
demanding that he should stay;
now she rues so deeply
she stopped him from riding away.
– And thus roams Ebbé Skammelsen on many stormy trails.

His mother offered him cushion and chair
and place at the table to dine;
his father asked him to go around
and pour the golden wine.

Ebbé poured wine for Adéluds,
she shone like a golden sprite;
and he became so sorrowful
whenever he looked at the bride.

There was Ebbé Skammelsen
he poured as time went on;
then he asked his father for leave
to rest himself and sit down.

There he sat for a little while,
until his mother said
that it might be the best for him,
if he would go to bed.

35 · Ebbé Skammelsen arose
with Adéluds on his arm;
verily, I tell you,
his heart felt hurt and harm.

Ebbé Skammelsen he asked,
out on the balcony:
"Do you remember, Adéluds,
you pledged me loyalty?"

"All the troth I got from God,
I gave to Peter, your brother;
I promise, all my living days
to care for you as a mother."
– And thus roams Ebbé Skammelsen on many stormy trails.

"I wooed you not for my mother,
I asked you to be my wife;
now shall Peter Skammelsen
pay for it with his life.

Harken to me, proud Adéluds,
together let's go away;
then I will kill my brother
and suffer for you this dismay."

40 · "If you take your brother's life,
you'll lose me, too, for sure;
and you shall grieve yourself to death
like a wild bird on the moor."

There was Ebbé Skammelsen
he drew his sword from his side,
turned to lady Adéluds
and killed his brother's bride.

Under his scarlet mantle
he hid the bloody sword;
then he went and stood before
his brother in the hall.

"Peter, my brother, get to your feet
and hie yourself to the bride;
too long she's sitting in her bed
longing for you at her side."

"Harken, Ebbé Skammelsen,
do not spoil for a fight;
I promise, brother dear, that you
may sleep with my bride tonight."
– And thus roams Ebbé Skammelsen on many stormy trails.

45 • There was Ebbé Skammelsen
the sword from his side he drew;
there was his brother Peter's head
he severed with a blow.

46 • He wounded his father grievously,
his mother lost a hand;
and thus roams Ebbé Skammelsen
on many wild trails in the land.
– And thus roams Ebbé Skammelsen on many stormy trails.

26 TORBEN'S DAUGHTER AND HIS SLAYER
The Smaller Stockholm Manuscript, 1641

So many children we were at home
– in the swale –
when our father went to his tomb.
– Comes dawn, and the dew she drifts over hill and dale.

One Sunday they shined both spear and sword,
on Monday in anger they rode abroad.

They left the forest, and to the North
Sir Torben was ploughing back and forth.

"Well, here's Sir Torben, so gay and fine;
I'll now have revenge for that kinsman of mine."

5 • "I'll give you my home, I'll give you my farm
and also my daughter, so pretty and warm."

"We haven't come for your house and sod,
– in the swale –
but we have come to take your blood."
– Comes dawn, and the dew she drifts over hill and dale.

And then they cut Sir Torben up
like leaves that fell from the tree top.

And then they rode to Sir Torben's place,
there stood his daughter with beauty and grace.

There stood his daughter so fair and grand
with golden goblets in her hands.

10 · She filled the goblets unto the brim
for her father's slayer and toasted him.

"Had I but known your goodness and mien,
your father's blood I'd never have seen."

"If you harmed him, if he is slain,
you have caused me the deepest pain."

"If I have done you wrong before,
you shall share my fortune for evermore."

He lifted her unto his charger's back
and wrapped around her his cape so black.

15 · And then they rode across the fen,
– in the swale –
she never saw her father again.
– Comes dawn, and the dew she drifts over hill and dale.

27 LAVE STISEN AND LADY ELINE

Recording from Scania, about 1600, compare No. 75

There was Lavé Stisen,
going to war was he;
so happy was Esbern Hövidsen
that he at home could be.
– *For her there was nothing but sorrow.*

"Harken, my little maiden,
the guard of my home you be;
you guard Lady Eliné,
the joy of my heart is she."

It was not much later,
maybe two days or three,
that Esbern Hövidsen started out
for Lady Eliné to see.

"Harken, proud Lady Eliné,
with favor you me behold
and let a shirt be cut for me,
embroidered nicely with gold."

5 · "If I let a shirt be cut for you,
embroidered nicely with gold,
that Lavé Stisen would never like,
when he about it was told.

If I let a shirt be cut for you
and hear about it would he,
if I embroidered it nicely with fur,
Lavé would surely kill me.

Never would I sorrow
and never shed a tear
didn't I expect Lavé Stisen
came home from the war this year."

There was Eliné's maiden
she writes a secret chit
and sends a messenger abroad
to reach Lavé Stisen with it.
– For her there was nothing but sorrow.

"There is a stag in the garden,
his hoof tears all apart,
he lures away proud Lady Eliné
who is the joy of your heart."

10 · There was Lavé Stisen
he quit the war and came home;
but to welcome him at the gate
Eliné she would not come.

Enters the little page-boy,
wearing his silvery knife:
"God's mercy with you, Lady Eliné,
this has endangered your life."

Enters another page-boy,
wearing his cloak so red:
"God's mercy with you, Lady Eliné,
Sir Lavé will see you dead."

There was proud Lady Eliné
she called her little maid:
"Lay out my silken headdress
and velvet gown on my bed."

Entered then Sir Lavé,
holding a spiky bit;
to help proud Lady Eliné
nobody now was fit.

15 · All the day he flogged her
and took it up again
the following day and continued
till Lady Eliné was slain.
– *For her there was nothing but sorrow.*

So long did Lavé flog her
and none could bring her aid,
but for Esbern Hövidsen
who ran to the door afraid.

"Harken, Esbern Hövidsen,
and this my question be:
Why have you lured proud Lady Eliné
and turned her away from me?"

The knights they met in a hard embrace
where torches spread their light;
there was nobody in the world
who dared to help the knights.

19 · Where their feet were standing
they cracked the solid stone;
where their hands were clutching
the flesh fell off the bones.
– *For her there was nothing but sorrow.*

28 CAROL ALGOTSON
Niels Christensen's Songbook, about 1729

Sir Carol left and went abroad,
betrothed a pretty maid;
now Carol shall never more be free,
in irons is he laid.
– *Sir Carol roams as an outlaw.*

Entered the first of Carol's brothers,
a better one never sees:
"Today I offer for Sir Carol
six hundred saddled steeds."
– *Sir Carol roams as an outlaw.*

Entered the second of Carol's brothers,
a brother in whom you'd rely:
"Today I offer for Sir Carol
my life, I am willing to die."

Entered the third of Sir Carol's brothers,
he offered more than them all:
"Today I offer for Sir Carol
both our church and stall."

5 · "Arise, all three of Carol's brothers,
God free you from anguish and fear;
but never shall you see the day
when Carol rides out from here."

Entered Sir Carol's father and mother,
knelt for the Danish king:
"Today we offer for Sir Carol
gold, oxen and everything."

Entered at last Sir Carol's betrothed,
she took the hat off her head:
"Today I offer for Sir Carol
to sleep with the king in his bed.

Riverisle and Vendelsisle
I'll give you with a will;
the drawbridge post is of narwhale bone,
the drawbridge of hardened steel.

Riverisle and Vendelsisle
for them you may yearn;
and you shall never see the day
you're offered a higher return."
– *Sir Carol roams as an outlaw.*

10 • "Arise, arise, proud Mettélil,
God free you from every harm;
but you shall never see the day
when Carol sleeps in your arm.

I went to bed one night to sleep,
I knew no danger nor strife;
entered Canute and young Sir Carol,
they wouldn't spare my life.

One shoe I still had in my hand,
one on my foot I wore;
Sir Carol did not know me
when I slipped out of the door.

By God's great help, as prisoner
Sir Carol is under my sway;
I hope to God on Heaven's throne,
Canute shall not get away."

Then they took Sir Carol
by his golden lock,
with an axe they beheaded him
in the prisoner's dock.

15 • Then the three brothers of Carol
the king they wanted to spite,
and they put the bloody trunk
up in the saddle to ride.

16 · Then the bride of Sir Carol
the king she wanted to harm,
and she raised the bloody head
and took it in her arms.
– *Sir Carol roams as an outlaw.*

29 THE WOMAN-MURDERER
Karen Brahe's Folio Manuscript, about 1583

Wolf he woos proud Venélil
– *but the linden tree grows* –
"Will you become my sweetheart dear?"
– *Don't heed that kind of counsel.*

"Lead you to an isle shall I,
where you shall live and never die.

Lead you to a land shall I,
where you shall never mourn or cry.

There grows no grass but bulb and root,
there sing no birds but owls that hoot.

5 · All the springs they run with wine,
do believe me, sweetheart mine."

"I do believe a young man's word,
but still the grass must grow on earth.

How shall I get away from home,
where everyone watches who cares for me?

My father and mother watch me,
also my sisters' husbands.

I'm also watched by my brothers eight,
may Jesus guard them early and late."

10 • "And even if everyone stood guard,
– but the linden tree grows –
you shall tonight with me depart."
– Don't heed that kind of counsel.

"How shall I get away with you
without them knowing what I do?"

"Proud Venélil, gather together your gold,
and I shall saddle my steed so bold.

You'll ride the steed that I shall hold,
and you shall wear my helmet of gold.

My golden sword around you I gird,
such style of a maiden was never heard."

15 • They rode along through the forest green,
on the saddle-bow was a golden sheen.

And when they came to a quiet dale,
Wolf he wanted to rest for a while.

Proud Venélil on the earth sat down,
Wolf dug a grave so deep in the ground.

"Listen, Wolf, and tell me yourself:
whom is the grave for that you delve?"

"For my horse it's too tight and slim,
and my little dog, too long for him."

20 • "You look yonder towards the town
from where the bloody streams run down.

Eight young maids there happened to be,
fairest I did ever see.

Eight young maidens I did woo,
– but the linden tree grows –
and afterwards them all I slew.
– Don't heed that kind of counsel.

And now the ninth it shall be you,
the penance for my sins you shall do."

Proud Venélil sat and pondered on
what answer would him best become.

25 · "For eight long years for me you did sue,
but never I did fondle you.

I always had a dream so fair,
I picked the lice out of your hair."

He rested his head in Venélil's lap,
his sleep it wasn't a pleasant nap.

She took from his neck the golden bands
and used them to tie up his hands.

And then she loosened the rope off his steed
and tied it securely around his feet.

30 · "Now, Wolf, wake up, wake up and speak,
I will not kill you in your sleep.

Now you shall see where stands the town
from where the bloody streams run down.

For eight young maidens did you sue,
and afterwards them all you slew.

And now the ninth one shall be you,
the penance for all their sins you'll do."

"Stop Venélil, don't kill me, nay!
– but the linden tree grows –
and you I never shall betray."
– Don't heed that kind of counsel.

35 • "Methink it still was great treachery
when here you wanted to undo me.

With hand and mouth you pledged your faith,
but still there was treachery beneath.

'tis the last time that you've laid
your snare for any trusting maid."

She drew his golden sword so bright,
and as to Wolf that served him right.

So womanly the sword she drew,
so manly with the sword she slew.

40 • "Wolf, wallow in blood, until you are dead,
but I am still so proud a maid."

41 • She mounted his steed and forged ahead,
– but the linden tree grows –
and she came home, so proud a maid.
– Don't heed that kind of counsel.

30 BIRTH IN THE GROVE
Recorded in Thy, Jutland, by A. C. Povlsen-Dal, 1855

Out on the floor Rose-Ella danced
so hard that the milk from her bosom sprang.
– now, now and how, how –
so hard that the milk from her bosom sprang.

"Hark, lovely daughter, hark, daughter so fine,
why springs the milk from the breasts of thine?
– *now, now and how, how* –
why springs the milk from the breasts of thine?"

"Oh, no, dear mother, it isn't milk,
it is of the mead I yesterday drank."

"No, brown is the mead and white the milk,
so milk and mead don't look alike."

5 · "It helps no longer to hide it from thee:
Sir Medvil he has tempted me."

"And if Sir Medvil has tempted thee,
no longer am I dear mother to thee.

Sir Medvil shall hang from the gallows tree,
below, on the stake shall I fasten thee."

Rose-Ella put on her mantle so red,
away to Sir Medvil's house she fled.

She tapped on the window with fingers so slim:
"Arise, Sir Medvil, and let me in."

10 · "No, nobody have I pledged a tryst,
and nobody enters my house tonight."

She tapped on the window with fingers so fine:
"I am Rose-Ella, sweetheart of thine.

I am Rose-Ella, sweetheart of thine,
and I have talked to the mother of mine.

And thou shalt hang on the gallows tree,
below, on the stake she will fasten me."

"No, I don't want to be hanged for thee,
and thou wilt not burn on the stake for me,
– *now, now and how, how* –
and thou wilt not burn on the stake for me."

15 • Sir Medvil saddles his dapple-grey steed
and asks Rose-Ella herself to seat.

And when they came to the rosy bosk't
to rest for a while Rose-Ella asked.

"The saddle is either far too tight
or else the road far too long for the ride?"

"The road is not too long for the ride,
although the saddle is far too tight."

Sir Medvil spreads out his cape so brown
and asks Rose-Ella to set her down.

20 • "O Christ, if I had just one of my maids
to help me a little in my straits."

"Thy maids they are far away from here,
they cannot help thee in thy despair.

Myself I will swath my head in skin,
myself I will be the midwife's stand-in."

"No, sooner I faint and give up my life,
ere man sees woman's distress and strife.

Oh, give me some water, a drop or two,
for that might lessen my heart's great woe."

25 • He went to fetch water in his silver-buckled shoe,
to his sweetheart he wanted to be true.

But when he had trod the road so long,
two nightingales sat and warbled a song,
– now, now and how, how –
two nightingales sat and warbled a song.

"Dead in the bosk Rose-Ella lies,
and two small sons she has at her side."

And when he came back to the rosy bosk,
then it was true what the birds had sung.

He dug a grave both deep and wide
and laid the three of them side by side.

30 · And when he laid them under the sod,
it seemed the children cried under his foot.

He placed his sword against a rock,
the sword point through his heart was struck.

32 · And now they know no woe nor plight,
Sir Medvil rests at Rose-Ella's side.
– now, now and how, how –
Sir Medvil rests at Rose-Ella's side.

31 SVEND IN THE ROSE GARDEN
Recording from South Sealand by Franziska Carlsen, 1846

"Where were you at this late hour
– Svend in the rose garden near?"
"I have been in the bower
– O my mother dear.
– I shall be late or never."

"Why is your sword so bloody?"
"Because I have killed my brother."

"Where will you turn your course?"
"I'll flee this country of ours."

"What will you do with your good wife
– *Svend in the rose garden near?"*
"She'll spin for her food and keep alive
– *O my mother dear.*
– *I shall be late or never."*

5 • "What will you do with the children of yours?"
"I shall place them with friends of ours."

"When shall we see your home-coming?"
"When women are all widow-women."

"When are they all widow-women?"
"When all the men are dead."

"When are all men dead?"
"When all farms are desolate."

"When are they desolate?"
"When ravens they grow white."

10 • "When do ravens grow white?"
"When the swans grow black."

"When do swans grow black?"
"When we see feathers sink."

"When will we see feathers sink?"
"When we see stones afloat."

"When will we see stones afloat?"
"When we see the ocean bloom."

14 • "When will the ocean bloom
– *Svend in the rose garden near?"*
"When we hear the crack of doom
– *O my mother dear.*
– *I shall be late or never."*

6 · HUMOR AND SADNESS

32 THE MAIDEN'S MORNING DREAM

Recorded near Lemvig, Jutland, by P. Kr. Madsen, 1870

Fair Vesterland was born at evening time
– *who tears the leaves off the lily* –
her mother was dead before early mass time.
– *She dances the dew off the meadow.*

Her father he rode so many a path,
he married Greyveggen, a stepmother bad.

She bestowed on her daughters honor so rich,
but bestowed on fair Vesterland strokes by a switch.

She bestowed on her daughters golden boons,
but bestowed on fair Vesterland swabs and brooms.

5 · Greyveggen entered through the door:
"Tell me the dream that you had this morn."

"I dreamt a little duck was I
that to the Wenders' land did fly.

I dreamt that strong and wide was my wing,
I'd rule the land for the Wenders' king."

"I curse you, fair maid, for the luck you've found."
And then she struck Vesterland dead to the ground.

"I curse you, fair maid, for the luck you've found;
in the yard the king and his Wenders dismount.

10 · You'll stand in the sight of the Wenders' king,
– who tears the leaves off the lily –
but not in your gold robe and golden ring."
– She dances the dew off the meadow.

"Why do you forbid me my gold to wear,
the gift from my mother, before you came here?

Why do you forbid me the gold so red,
I came into it when my mother was dead?"

She went to the chest where her gold she hid,
she used all her strength and opened the lid.

Then she put gold on top of gold,
all that her fingers and arms could hold.

15 · Her golden scissors she took in her hand,
in sight of the Wenders' king she did stand.

"Oh, tell me, fair Vesterland, without fail,
why are your cheeks so wan and pale?"

"Last night I fell from the balustrade
from up above, and hurt my head."

"No, your hard-hearted stepmother wouldn't unbend,
she struck you dead before my advent.

What must be cut or sewn or bound?
It ill befits you to go to town."

20 · He wrapped her into a beautiful cloak,
the road to the Wenders' land they took.

21 · He crowned her and put her on the throne,
– who tears the leaves off the lily –
for she was to rule as his very own.
– She dances the dew off the meadow.

33 THE DICE GAME
Songbook from Als, about 1700, compare No. 76

In the yard of the king there stood a bold knight
– *roses and lilies of the valley* –
and soon a fair maiden came in sight
– *the servants they weren't* –
and soon a fair maiden came in sight
– *the servants they couldn't dally.*

"Fair maiden, fair maiden, throw dice with me,
I'll wager my tallest hat against thee."

"Thy tallest hat I surely shall get,
with my finest gloves I shall call thy bet."

The first time the dice on the table were tossed,
fair maiden she won and the knight he lost.

5 · "Fair maiden, fair maiden, throw dice with me,
I'll wager my saddle and horse against thee."

"Thy saddle and horse I shall surely get,
with my golden slippers I'll call thy bet."

The next time the dice on the table were tossed,
fair maiden she won and the knight he lost.

"Fair maiden, fair maiden, throw dice with me,
I'll wager my seven ships against thee."

"Thy seven ships I surely shall get,
with my golden crown I shall call thy bet."

10 · The third time the dice on the table were tossed,
fair maiden she won and the knight he lost.

The knight went out and looked towards the sky
– *roses and lilies of the valley* –
with woe in his heart and tears in his eye
– *the servants they weren't* –
with woe in his heart and tears in his eye
– *the servants they couldn't dally.*

The knight he prayed on his bended knee:
"O Lord, my Master, throw dice with me."

From Heaven sounded a voice: "Arise,
arise, bold knight, keep on throwing dice."

"Fair maiden, fair maiden, throw dice with me,
I'll wager my marble-white neck against thee."

15 • "Your marble-white neck I surely shall get,
with my honor and troth I shall call thy bet."

The fourth time the dice on the table were tossed,
the knight he won and the fair maiden lost.

"Bold knight, I can play against you no more,
my golden crown you must settle for."

No lad who is honorable and bold
should barter a maiden's honor for gold.

19 • He pledged her, and then he rode with the maid
– *roses and lilies of the valley* –
to his home and placed her in his bed
– *the servants they weren't* –
to his home and placed her in his bed
– *the servants they couldn't dally.*

34 THE DEAR ROBE
Queen Sofia's Manuscript, 1584

There was a pretty damsel,
she strolls in the glade alone;
a handsome swain he crosses her road
among the grass and stones.
– *Aye, on a summer morning.*

"Well met, I greet you, handsome swain,
who to this glade was led;
please, take your robe and also mine
and make us of them a bed."

"I shan't spread my robe beneath you,
it's made of velvet green;
if it once became wet in the dew,
it would shrink in every seam.

I shan't spread my robe beneath you,
of velvet it is sewn;
I bought it for fifteen marks the ell
when I was in Stockholm town."

5 · "My mother she lives up north in town,
of bolsters she has two;
please, wait here for me, handsome swain,
while I fetch one that will do.

My mother lives up north in town,
of bolsters she has ten;
please, wait here for me, handsome swain,
while I fetch one of them."

She then threw his robe around his head,
asked him to wait right there;
she went off and didn't come back,
tricked him, that wasn't fair.

She threw his robe around his head,
asked him to wait for a while;
she went off and didn't come back,
she treated the swain with guile.
– *Aye, on a summer morning.*

Away the pretty damsel went,
she laughed with glee and mirth;
her robe was made of golden cloth,
the train swept across the earth.

10 · He stayed for a day, he stayed for two
and waited for the maid;
she didn't come to the grassy glade
with covers for their bed.

There he stood from Easter
and until Whitsuntide;
but to see the maid in the church
he dared not go nor ride.

Then he saw and met the maid
outside the chapel door:
"Pray, what became of our common wish,
and why was the end so poor?"

"Why, you can thank your robe for that,
of velvet it was sewn;
you bought it for fifteen marks the ell,
when you were in Stockholm town.

Yes, you can thank your robe for that,
which you so highly esteem;
if it once became wet in the dew,
it would shrink in every seam.

15 · Harken, master Magnus,
my word is true and fair:
I offered you a royal gift,
but no, you did not dare.
– *Aye, on a summer morning.*

16 · If a damsel had met me,
and I was a swain like you,
and had my robe been of golden cloth,
it would have been soaked in the dew."
– *Aye, on a summer morning.*

35 SISTER WOOS BROTHER
Anna Basse's Manuscript, before 1616

Together they sat with passionate love,
a sister and her brother;
I never knew of two of their kind
who better could court each other.
– *The forest is already blooming.*

"Would Christ you were the handsomest knight
who ever went out for a ride;
then I would be a sword of gold
and hang at the nobleman's side."

"Oh, it is bad to be a sword
and hang at the nobleman's side;
many a drunkard is around
who'll unsheathe the sword and fight."

"Would Christ you were the handsomest maple
that ever grew in the wood;
then I would be a blade of grass
and stand at the maple's root."

5 · "Oh, it is bad to be the grass
that stands at the maple's root;
many a maiden walks among trees
and crushes it under her foot."
– *The forest is already blooming.*

"Would Christ you were the handsomest stag
that played in the wood without fear;
then I would be a little doe
and frolic beside the deer."

"Oh, it is bad to be a doe
and frolic beside the deer;
the hunter rides so oft in the wood
and unchains his pointers there."

"Would Christ you were the handsomest church
that stood on a lonely site;
then I would be the altar of gold,
prepared in the church for the rite."

"Oh, it is bad to be an altar,
prepared in the church for the rite;
many a paltry soul dwells there
under the shield of the night."

10 · "Would Christ you were the handsomest pond
as ever was seen before;
then I would be a little duck
and swim from shore to shore."

"Oh, it is bad to be a duck
and swim from shore to shore;
the hawk that flies high up in the sky
would pounce and away he would soar."

"Would Christ you were the handsomest reed
that stood on the hill slope wide;
then I would be a blade of grass
that stood with the reed, at its side."
– *The forest is already blooming.*

"Oh, it is bad to be the grass
that stands with the reed, at its side;
the shepherd drives his cattle out
to grass on the hill slope wide.

14 · You travel east, and I travel west,
to the end of the world, we two;
and you shall never see the day
when I shall send for you."
– *The forest is already blooming.*

36 THE YOUNG MAN'S DREAM
Svaning's Manuscript I, about 1580

In bed I lay one night and dreamed
of her for whom I pine;
I thought I felt her in my arms
right at that very time.
– *I wish to God that some day she will be mine.*

Quickly I turned around in sleep
to hold that rose of mine;
the rose was gone, and I was alone,
and wildly my heart did pine.

So many there are all over the world
who suffer this great harm;
I hope to God I shall see the day
I'll press her in my arm.

So many there are all over the world
who suffer this great plight;
I hope to God I shall see the day
when she lies at my side.
– *I wish to God that some day she will be mine.*

5 · So many there are all over the world
who hope it will never be;
I hope to God I shall see the day
I'll bring her home with me.

All day she's ever in my mind,
at night in my dreams she's set;
would God that soon she might be mine,
or else that I'd forget.

7 · Then help me, God, with all your might
and cause it to occur:
O grant that she in truth be mine,
for I know I am worthy of her.
– *I wish to God that some day she will be mine.*

37 THE MAIDEN'S COMPLAINT
Broadside, about 1800

The world is full of deceit and stealth,
of that you are often aware,
it clings to poverty and to wealth,
where do you find troth and care?
– *But the graveyard hides our sorrows.*

The apple hangs never so high on bough
that some time it will not fall,
whoever has a devoted friend
should love him better than all.

Once I had gotten the dearest friend,
I thought of nobody else,
his words they sounded ever so sweet,
but in his heart he was false.
– *But the graveyard hides our sorrows.*

If only that heart of his had been worth
as much as the words he did say,
from him then nobody in the world
could have turned my heart away.

5 • A council was held by the evil tongues,
our friendship they wanted to kill,
albeit the highest council belongs
to God and reigns by His will.

There's never a sting that knows how to pierce
as the heart of a man gone wrong,
there's never a snare that's any more fierce
than a human, deceitful tongue.

Now I am like a motherless child
and a child whose father is gone:
when others rejoice in dancing and play,
all friendship leaves me alone.

Now I am like the lonesome tree
that stands on a desolate moor
away from town, from shelter and lee
and is so unhappy and poor.

Now I am like a bird in distress
that sits in a lonely cleft
and sobs by herself and sorrows to death
for the mate of whom she's bereft.

10 • Now I am like a fish in the seine,
while others gambol in glee
deep down on the ocean bed, I remain
imprisoned by perfidy.
– *But the graveyard hides our sorrows.*

11 • You crush me, oh, secret languishment
too heavy a burden for me:
he who before made me glad and content
has brought me great misery.
– *But the graveyard hides our sorrows.*

II · HUMOR

7 · JOCULAR SONGS

38 THE WEDDING OF THE FLY

Broadside, late 18th century; compare No. 77

A New Song about the Wedding of the Gnat **and** *the Fly,*
and Their Poor Fate Caused by the Wasp **and** *the Bee.*

The gnat pulls in his feelers blue
– *cum pi, cum pa, cum padrian* –
it is wee fly-farm he travels to
– *cum pi caritu, fatitasia.*

And when he came to wee fly-farm,
the fly was donning her boots so warm.

"Tell me, wee fly, that I shan't quail,
when shall we get married, without fail?"

"Our wedding shall be some day in Fall,
when flies are plentiful, big and small."

5 · And there was pomp in the wedding house,
there danced a flea and there jumped a louse.

A stranger sight I never saw,
there danced a louse with sword all drawn.

Out on the floor stepped seven ants
and turned around in a stately dance.

The gnat knocked down wee fly so fair
– cum pi, cum pa, cum padrian –
and dragged her across the floor by her hair.
– cum pi caritu, fatitasia.

She got to her feet, and tears she shed:
"Was that what you promised, before we were wed?"

10 · Four ants arose and stood in the middle,
they hummed on their basses and played a fiddle.

Then joined by an inch-worm, newly born,
they sang by note and blew a horn.

The wasp and the bee were on the fell,
they wanted to know where the wedding was held.

They pledged each other brotherhood
and flew to the place where the wedding stood.

When they got in, the wasp and the bee,
those who were blind, began to see.

15 · For when they got in, they demanded here
the tax and debt from yesteryear.

They punched and they stung with all their might,
till ants and flies said a quick good-night.

Neither tax nor debts of yesteryear
they got, for ants and flies disappeared.

18 · Just let them lie and rest their scruff,
– cum pi, cum pa, cum padrian –
for the ants and flies have had quite enough.
– cum pi caritu, fatitasia.

39 THE BANQUET OF THE BIRDS
Recording from Jutland by Evald Tang Kristensen

There was in the forest a party so gay,
it was for the eagle, so old and so grey,
and all his children young, 'midst nightingale song
and joy on every other little birdie's tongue.

"Oh, long have I lived in matrimonial state,
but then I became a widower of late."
He thought with clever mien his council to convene
and make them choose for him another mate and queen.

Now he was an eagle, and she was a kite,
both of them were hungry and wanted a bite.
"If me you will obey, we will invite, I say,
both rich and poor, we mustn't turn anyone away."

The magpie went for all and sundry to invite,
she ran from dawn to dusk and was a common sight:
"With greetings from my lord, who asks if you'll afford
the honor on him to partake in food from our board."

5 · First was the raven asked their minister to be,
in his black coat there was no better choice than he;
he was a cultured gent, a wise and witless mind,
a preacher of his kind you'll very seldom find.

The starling he was next, as deacon he would do,
he always sang by ear and knew a thing or two;
with voice he, too, was blessed and sang his very best,
his throat was clean and wholesome, and healthy was his chest.

And in the modest crow an able cook they saw,
who never used to eat the victuals that were raw;
she didn't waste or spoil, she knew the work and toil,
she only needs to watch the pot to know when it will boil.

They had two music makers, and they were mighty wee,
whom else than the swallow and the skylark could it be?
a minuet they played, so people's nerves got frayed,
it mattered not how little the lightest of them weighed.

The music makers got neither nickels nor dimes,
though music makers also need money at times;
they're neither strong nor stern, and disrespect they earn,
well, be it as it may, but they were forced to take their turn.

10 • Again they asked the council to tell them whom they should
select for the position to carry in the food,
one who had tact and will, experience and skill
and didn't stumble over his own feet and slop and spill.

The stork shall be the waiter, for he is strong and straight
and knows about the business to cater and to wait;
his voice is dignified: "Shall it be boiled or fried?
Whatever you desire you shall not be denied."

He brought the chicken soup, it was a pretty treat,
for in it was the fat and delicious chicken meat.
The crow who was ingrate and wily, didn't wait,
but grabbed into the pot and placed it on her plate.

The hawk sat next to her, and he began to scold:
"You got the job to cater for the party, I am told;
but now you act and do, as were it all for you,
and you deserve a hiding till you are black and blue."

The crow got raving mad, right to the very core,
and thought for sure that she wouldn't stand for any more;
for she began to shout: "I'll teach him whom to flout,
I'll kill the haughty hawk, I'll teach him to be proud."

15 • The eagle sat and listened to this blustering affair,
and to the crow he said: "You are so full of steam and air;
don't bother about that, he'll throw you on the mat,
tell him that you are sorry and then take off your hat."

The crow she wouldn't listen to counsel of this kind,
to grabble with the hawk was what she had in mind:
"Come on, old woman-knight, and you shall have a fight,
and I will show you, if to play with me was right."

The hawk and the crow they jousted and they clashed,
the crow lay on the ground, prostrated and smashed;
she to the eagle cries, tears overflow her eyes:
"I was a fool as I didn't follow your advice.

Oh, listen, bridegroom dear, please hurry to my aid,
he stings my sinful body, and I am much afraid,
his talons are so long, and they are very strong,
he pinches me with them as with a pair of tongs."

Just inside the door sat the owl as a guest,
he ate of the dishes that he thought tasted best;
he gorged himself so much as he never did before,
that he in the end couldn't swallow any more.

20 • The poor owl was greedy and continued to eat
and filled himself to the brim with pigs' feet
and started to complain it was a harder strain
than ever he had had, of stomach ache and pain.

The preacher asked the owl: "Please tell me, my friend,
if you do really think, you'll get well in the end?"
"No, I must surely face what's going to take place,
that soon I must get buried, as numbered are my days."

He turned away his head as archly as can be,
because old rogues like this you can't take seriously;
and in a teasing mood he said: "You don't feel good,
I see the salty sweat drops seeping through your hood."

The eagle said to him: "Let's have your wedding toast,"
and grandly handed him four pennies, at the most;
but that was not enough, they held him by the scruff
and took his Sunday clothes as security for the stuff.

They put him on a horse, he wasn't used to ride,
and therefore like a sack to the horseback he was tied;
that wasn't very smart and upset the applecart,
at every little jiggle of the horse he let a fart.

25 • His wife thought she would get some titbits from the spread,
she smelled him long before she eyes upon him laid;
his pants were full of what they really hadn't ought,
he'd liked to hide his troubles, but that he managed not.

"Now, listen, goodwife dear, I ask you to be nice,
I do not want to go on any junket in a trice;
I pawned my coat, I did, and most of all my kit,
for I was short of money, had just a little bit."

"What did you do with all the money thrown about
and with your Sunday clothes that you are now without?"
His answer was right coarse: "No business of yours;
that I have all forgotten while riding on the horse."

His wife she got so angry over this gruff remark,
about how things were going she was left in the dark;
she grabbed him by his locks, gave him some hefty knocks:
"I'll teach you in the future to act wiser than an ox."

[The misbegotten owl he begged to let him be,
the wife she didn't want to listen to his plea,]

and after him she went, until his skin was rent,
and then he had to thank her for the gracious punishment.

30 · In the eyes of the eagle the owl stood high and wide,
when he showed his masterpiece and shed his broken hide
and had it made into a coat and a chapeau
to suit him if he out on another spree should go.

31 · Now, nothing happened more at the banquet to tell,
as the owl had paid for everything all by himself;
they ate and drank – oh my! – and their pipe smoke hid the sky,
and three days after they broke up and said good-bye.

40 THE MASTER'S COUNSEL
Vibeke Bild's Greater Folio Manuscript, 1646 ff

A brand-new poem you shall hear
– *jump briskly about* –
if you will learn and lend me your ear
– *lalalirum* –
about a swain
who did complain
about his plight to his master and friend.
– *lalalirum.*

"O master, who are wise and just,
whom I am fully prepared to trust:
Ahead or behind
I always find
the question of wedlock in my mind.

And thus I beg you in honesty
that you for me a teacher will be,
that you will state
whom I shall rate
worthwhile to be my wife and mate."

Answered the master, wise and discreet,
– *jump briskly about* –
who knew full well how to write and read:
– *lalalirum* –
"My dear, young man,
my knowledge scan,
I'll counsel you the best I can.
– *lalalirum.*

5 • If you in this wide world set out
to see what it is all about,
then let me tell:
both poor and swell
you meet, and young and old as well.

Don't marry up with one who's old,
she'll spy in every nook and fold;
no, old and young
don't get along,
they pull each way in the harness thong.

Despite her wealth you shouldn't seek
the rich one out, if she isn't meek;
for many do
wholeheartedly rue
they married for wealth, in a year or two.

She who is poor and woebegone
brings in her marriage misery on;
a hungry tooth,
I say forsooth,
makes marriage anything but smooth.

Besides, be sure to keep in mind:
the wicked you must leave behind;
for don't you see,
such one as she
can make the greatest misery.

10 · A fool the man is always called
– *jump briskly about* –
who can't make out 'tween virtue and fault;
– *lalalirum* –
a spavined nag
is a sorry drag
to buy, to that you turn your back.
– *lalalirum.*

Select a wife with honesty,
virtuous, deaf, who cannot see;
take my advice,
and use your eyes,
one of that kind will amply suffice."

"Oh, master, I'm confused and implore
that you'll explain your counsel some more;
you said before
I would deplore,
if she should happen to have a flaw."

Answered the master with clever mind:
"She must be one whose eyes are blind,
that she won't peer
with avid leer
quite unashamedly here and there.

She shan't know how to hear with her ears
from others, what immoral appears;
bad whoring song
and an evil tongue
did often many husbands wrong.

15 · And she must never be inclined
to take men's gifts of any kind;
she'll get the blame
and a bad name;
for such a one you must never aim.

And she must also have crippled feet
– *jump briskly about* –
that can't run up and down the street,
– *lalalirum* –
unchaste, untrue,
with dance and brew
and whoop it up at a jolly do.
– *lalalirum.*

Dumb shall she be of mouth and tongue
and never sing a whoring song,
must not traduce,
lie or confuse,
and scurvy talk she mustn't use.

As bells are valued for their tone,
so by her song a whore is known;
so use your head
when you get wed,
for marriage later can't be shed.

The last advice that you shall hear:
in decency select your peer,
and do not rue,
but make it do,
what God and fortune will bring to you."

20 • "Oh, thank you, thanks a thousandfold,
– *jump briskly about* –
dear master, for what you have told;
– *lalalirum* –
now we shall see,
what it may be,
that God and fortune will render me."
– *lalalirum.*

41 A BETTER BARGAIN

Vibeke Bild's Greater Folio Manuscript, 1646 ff

A lad proposed to a maid so bright:
"Won't you be bedded with me tonight?"
– *We're treading the dance together.*

"No, I don't want to, if as much gold
were given to me as our church can hold."

"Be quiet, sweet maid, don't say the like,
a better bargain we still may strike.

A better bargain we still may strike,
we'll get you for some clothes you like."

5 · A lad proposed to a maid so bright:
"Won't you be bedded with me tonight?"

"No, I don't want to, if as much gold
were given to me as our vestry can hold."

"Be quiet, sweet maid, don't say the like,
a better bargain we still may strike.

A better bargain we still may strike,
we'll get you for some shoes you like."

A lad proposed to a maid so bright:
"Won't you be bedded with me tonight?"

10 · "No, I don't want to, if as much gold
were given to me as my chest can hold."

"Be quiet, sweet maid, don't say the like,
a better bargain we still may strike.

A better bargain we still may strike,
we'll get you for some gloves you like."
– *We're treading the dance together.*

A lad proposed to a maid so bright:
"Won't you be bedded with me tonight?"

"No, I don't want to, if as much gold
were given to me as my thimble can hold."

15 • "Be quiet, sweet maid, don't say the like,
a better bargain we still may strike.

A better bargain we still may strike,
we'll get you for two pins or something alike."

17 • "Had I my mistress' needle not lost,
I wouldn't have sold my maidenhood thus."
– *We're treading the dance together.*

42 THE LAD WHO WAS FOOLED
Recording from Jutland by Evald Tang Kristensen

A knight so bold and a maid so gay
were going out to harvest hay.
– *And how she did laugh!*

After a joust with the hay that they ted
he hoed together a wedding bed.

"Now may I do what I want to do,
for I have made a bed for you?"

"Yes, you may do what you want to do,
but only if to my room we go."

5 · The knight he started to fuss and fume
and helped her getting back to her room.
– *And how she did laugh!*

"Now may I do what I want to do,
for back to your room I have taken you?"

"Yes, you may do what you want to do,
when out of my frock you have helped me, too."

The knight he started to fuss and fume
and helped her with her frock in her room.

"Now may I do what I want to do,
for with your frock I assisted you?"

10 · "Yes, you may do what you want to do,
when out of my shift you have helped me, too."

The knight he started to fuss and fume
and helped her with her shift in her room.

"Now may I do what I want to do,
for with your shift I assisted you?"

"Yes, you may do what you want to do,
when up in my bed you have helped me, too."

The knight he started to fuss and fume
and helped her getting to bed in her room.

15 · "Now may I do what I want to do,
for into your bed I assisted you?"

"Yes, you may do what you want to do,
when out of my sark you have helped me, too."

The knight he started to fuss and fume
and helped her out of her sark in her room.
– *And how she did laugh!*

"Now may I do what I want to do,
for with your sark I assisted you?"

"Yes, you may do what you want to do,
but first go out, I must ask of you."

20 • The knight went out as he was told,
she shut the door with lock and bolt.

21 • With lock and bolt she shut the door:
"The devil should let you in any more."
– *And how she did laugh!*

43 PEASANT'S WIFE VISITS COURTIER
Ida Giöe's Manuscript, about 1630

The peasant and his woman
– *tread so lightly* –
they went to bed and talked a lot,
and it was all about me.

And when the peasant's eyes were closed,
his woman from his bed arose,
and then she went to me.

The peasant woke and looked around,
his pretty wife he never found,
for then she was with me.

The peasant donned his coat so warm
and looked for her all o'er the farm,
and now she was with me.

5 · He looked in field and house,
– *tread so lightly* –
but never he found his spouse,
because she was with me.

The woodpile then he tried for luck:
"Maybe my woman here is stuck."
Later she went from me.

And he put on another gown
and looked around all over town;
and then she was with me.

"And if I knew where she might be,
then I would serve her obediently,
although she went from me."

Came he to the mere,
his goodwife met him there;
then she came from me.

10 · "Be welcome, wife, so pretty and fine;
where hast thou been in the night time?"
And since she went from me.

"I have been minding our affairs,
I went out and moved our mares.
And later I went from thee.

I went into the grassy lands,
and I awakened our hands."
Right then she awakened me.

"And I was quite far away,
I showed our farmhands how to rake hay."
'Twas then she raked with me.

"I was down at the river side
– *tread so lightly* –
to show our hands where to use the scythe."
All the time she made love to me.

15 • He gave her a hug so slyly and fain:
"Thou art always thinking of our gain,
when thou goest away from me."

He patted her on her cheek so white:
"Thou always dost what I think is right
when thou art away from me."

She gave him slyly a hug so kind:
"Heaven gave thee a clever mind,
that I can see of thee.

18 • I do not talk in a mocking mood,
– *tread so lightly* –
thou surely canst tell the bad from the good,
when thus I go from thee."

44 THE BIG CROW
Recording from Funen by H. C. Frydendahl, 1942

Dad also sang the ditty about the big crow, but I don't remember it all. I never cared for it. It is just nonsense. I only know bits of it.

A peasant went out on his field to reap
– *trallera lalala trallera lalala* –
and shot a crow that was fast asleep.
– *falleri fallera tralalalala.*

Later a note from the bishop he got:
"What did you do with the crow you shot?"

"The crow was useful for many things . . ."
– *trallera lalala trallera lalala* –
Here she stopped and said: Then comes something I don't want to repeat.
– *falleri fallera tralalalala.*

"The head I made into a chapel pew,
the beak I used as a spout for my brew.

5 · The eyes I used for a window pane,
it brightens the room as a torch aflame.

And all my rope from the guts I strung,
the feet I used as a fork for the dung.

I thatched with the feathers a good-sized house,
a perfect shield against rat and mouse.

The bones I used for my master's boat,
the very best that was ever afloat.

9 · The hindpart I made into a stein . . . ."
– *trallera lalala trallera lalala* –
She added: Well, it was another word, but let us say hindpart.
"Come now, my friends, drink plenty of wine."
– *falleri fallera tralalalala.*

45 UPSIDE DOWN DITTY
Langebek's Quarto Manuscript, 1562

The wolf he rests in the stable,
he has the bit in his mouth;
the horse he roams upon the sea
widely from north to south.
– *The horses crow, while the chickens ride.*

The horses roam upon the sea,
widely from north to south;
the pike she flies way up in the sky.
– *The horses crow, while the chickens ride.*

The pikes they fly way up in the sky,
they drop a feather wherever they fly;
the wolf he sits on the chapel's top.

The wolf he sits on the chapel's top,
the pidgeon eats the little lamb up;
I've come to a house of the highest rank.

5 • I've come to a house of the highest rank,
where abbots burned and candles sang;
and out I peek and in I look.

And out I peek and in I look,
a hag is sitting in a nook,
she combs the porridge and stirs the flax.

She combs the porridge and stirs the flax,
the bald-headed maids unfold their locks;
here sings the dumb and dances the lame.

Here sings the dumb and dances the lame,
the blind embroiders on her frame;
I've seen it with my very own eyes.

I've seen it with my very own eyes
that inside the priest the chapel lies;
the deacon he fusses around outside.

10 • The moon lies in the heather stack,
the cur shines far and near;
I oiled my horse and saddled my boots,
no more would I tarry here.
– *The horses crow, while the chickens ride.*

III · LATER SONGS

8 · CREED AND SUPERSTITION

46 THE TEN MAIDENS' SONG
Joachim Moltke: Spiritual Handbook, 1639

The kingdom of Heaven is likened to
ten maidens with charm and address
who were betrothed to the Son of God
who reigns o'er salvation and bliss.
– *God pity all of us sinners.*

He went away to a foreign land
about his business
and bade them all to be at hand
according to his wish.

"Keep watch and pray by daylight and moon,
be ready with all that you own;
for don't forget I'll be here soon,
the hour shall not be known."

He went away, they didn't know where,
their hearts were heavy and sad;
five of them didn't tarry there,
their longing was too great.

5 · When it was almost midnight time,
and it was quiet all o'er,
they heard a voice like a mighty chime
that said: "O Lord, o Lord!

Come out, come out, you ten good maids,
this is your bridegroom's return,
provided you have your lanterns ablaze,
fed by your oil to burn."
– *God pity all of us sinners.*

To the five maidens both wise and good,
each with her lamp alight,
the foolish ones said: "We pray that you would
give us some oil to make bright."

"You better hurry and buy some more
that none of us shall be lacking."
The bridegroom hurried through the door,
the five they followed after.

The door was closed with greatest speed,
with rest and joy in there;
the other five hurried forth, indeed,
were caught by great despair.

10 • "O Lord, open up, O Master so grand,
we came as fast as we could;
we have complied with your command,
we hope that help us it would."

"Begone, begone, for I know you not,
you did not heed my call;
to walk in darkness shall be your lot,
without any joy at all."

12 • So let us change our mind and abide
and pray for our Master's ruth,
and let us forsake all worldly pride,
it profits us little, in truth.
– *God pity all of us sinners.*

47 JERUSALEM'S COBBLER
Niels Christensen's Songbook, about 1729

Oh, think of the salvation,
you Christian soul and heart,
that Christ through his privation
did to us all impart.
Let all our thoughts dwell on
the past when He consented
to have himself tormented
and died for everyone.

The Lord had set the hour
to crush the Jewish state;
Tiberius's power
Israel knew was great.
Still Jacob did condemn
the Saviour to be slain
with insult and disdain
right in Jerusalem.

I, Ahasuerus, used
to live as cobbler there;
the Master I accused
and loudly did declare:
"This man of mutiny,
seducer and insurgent
you crucify – it's urgent –
now on the gallows tree."

The death sentence just passed,
when Christ He bore the cross,
by gall and spite harassed
I saw Him near to us.
He wanted there to rest,
what He so highly needed;
I yelled to Him to beat it
at once as He could best.

5 · All mercy's godly charms
my wife and I forgot;
I carried in my arms
a small and tender tot.
Jesus away I sent
in my impatient ire:
"What do you here desire?
Go, take your punishment."

Christ heard my hue and cry,
His voice was weak and hoarse,
He was exhausted by
the burden of the cross.
He turned to me: "I say
to you, O Jew, start roaming
with agony and moaning
right until Judgment's Day."

To Golgotha I went
together with the crowd.
Soon after I was bent
on roaming and set out.
Before the path I trod,
I saw Him agonized;
but still He sacrificed
for Man His precious blood.

Right there caroused and vied
the savage Jewish crowd,
while sun and moon they sighed
at our Saviour's shout.
The sky was grey like lead,
I heard the mountain sob,
the Earth it opened up
when Jesus Christ lay dead.

I turned around in fright
at once and beat my chest.
The Lord knows well my plight,
sorely by sin distressed.
How many pains and tears
that I have suffered from,
oft to my mind they come
through seventeen hundred years.

10 · And thus at once I went
abroad as He decreed;
no clothes and not a cent
and neither food nor mead.
It hurt me all through life:
there wasn't time that I
might say a sad good-bye
to children and to wife.

Like an abandoned boat
I roam and drift about,
dressed in the same old coat,
never to be worn out.
I have no gold supplies,
for so He has decreed:
the Maker fills my need
in secret, otherwise.

So many an alien shore
repentantly I trod,
of many a country's lore
I understand a lot.
Jerusalem stood firm,
but last the town I found
prostrated to the ground,
just like a smothered worm.

I walked my way through Britain
and also Brittany
in days of yore, all smitten
with weary misery.
I found my way through Gaul,
Italy, Spain and Russia,
Greece, Netherlands and Prussia,
Moscow and Portugal.

I know how a Chaldean
and Hebrew must endure,
a Greek and an Armenian
around the river Kur.
No rest for me is meant
in desert, wood or lea,
no sleep will come to me,
I wander and repent.

15 • I went on weary tours
to Cracow and Berlin,
and then I changed my course
for Rostock and Stettin.
I saw great Lubeck's spell,
Hamburg and Wismar towns;
they kept beneath their gowns
a strange material.

I saw how men, baptized,
wallowed in evil's flood,
more than an anti-Christ
who doesn't know of God.
With powder in their hair
and painted everyone;
about what once went on
of old, they didn't care.

I heard with grief so sore
right many a bloody oath
that cut me to the core
and made my soul so loath.
Beware, O Man, beware,
His pain you shall not curse
that saved both you and yours
from every evil snare.

Of Christ's laments and throes
for you I can recite,
and of His thousand woes
and pains before He died.
Of Jews defying God
I'm an etern example;
and He erased their temple
because of Jesu blood.

19 • O Lord, you know that I
have always been unstaid;
help me to triumph by
your Holy Spirit's aid.
Give me your hand divine
that I be saved at last
with judgment on me passed
that honor's crown be mine.

Finis. The End.
May God His Mercy Send.
Niels Christensen, Starup Nygaard Eghd,
January 8 Anno 1729.

48 THE MAID WHO TROD ON THE LOAF
Broadside "Printed this year", end of 18th century

A peculiar story about what took place in a little town in Pomerania, named Sibbo, in the month of August, with regard to a poor servant girl on account of her disobedience to her poor parents, as well as to her great vanity.

Good people, I shall sing a song
about an awful wonder;
and it took place not long ago,
about it we must ponder.
Not long ago it came to pass
at Sibbo town, its place it has
way down in Pomerania.

A peasant poor was living there,
of children he had many;
just as the needy must do here,
they begged for bread and pennies.
But then his oldest daughter went
away from home and folks, intent
on entering into service.

The same became so full of pride
when on her own discretion,
she wallowed always, day and night,
in sin and in perdition.
For every penny that she earned
next day she into finery turned
and a vainglorious living.

Her master counseled her: "Dear maid,
your vanity eschew.
Look, we are not possessed by pride,
can that be said of you?
What you may save out of your pay,
give to your father dear, I pray,
who goes around a-begging."

5 · She said: "I'm pretty as can be,
far more than many others;
in secret many sigh for me,
so why should I not bother
with mirrors and the latest style
and finery that is worth my while
and that I work and pay for?"

But later on it came to pass
her father passed away;
her mother now a widow was,
in need and in dismay.
She turned to her and asked her aid,
that he might in his grave be laid,
if she could spare some money.

Now she had served for fourteen years,
when this event transpired;
her mother asked for help in tears,
help needed and desired.
Her daughter's answer was severe:
"You will obtain no money here;
him you yourself must bury.

I'll go to market without fail
for something nice to wear,
that very seldom is for sale
in stores both here and there."
'Twas then her mistress understood
that mercy no-one ever could
get from the wicked daughter.

The mistress was compassionate
when she the story heard
and gave ten thalers to the maid
to have her dad interred.
Without remorse, without a thought
the maid went out, the grave was bought,
and he was buried in it.

10 • Once she was asked at a christening
godmother to become;
two loaves her mistress told her bring
along to her mother's home.
She primped herself in highest glee,
and she behaved quite shamefully,
as you shall hear me tell you.

For as the shoes she wore were new,
she wanted them safeguarded;
she punished was for this, as you
right now shall have imparted.
She threw the loaves into the mud
and put her feet on them and trod –
oh, that was bad and sinful.

She only wished to save her shoes,
she didn't want them splattered;
the loaves of bread, made for the use
of people, little mattered.
God interfered immediately,
as everyone around could see;
she couldn't move a muscle.

She turned herself from side to side,
but something seemed to hold her;
she cried, but couldn't take a stride,
was frozen like a boulder.
And people streamed from dale and hill
to see the mighty miracle,
always to be remembered.

And everybody looked with fright
as no-one needs explain.
Three days she stood there, day and night,
as fettered by a chain.
A dreary desert did appear
round her, and none could venture near,
and she was frozen to it.

15 · And when the pastor heard where she
unhappily did languish,
he went to her immediately
to save her from her anguish.
To tears and sobbing she gave in
and readily confessed her sin;
but still the maid was punished.

She cried aloud: "Good people, see,
I am a great transgressor;
pray God He merciful will be,
my punishment make lesser.
For many a-one begs for his bread,
but with my foot I dared to tread
on Heaven's glorious handsel."

The people sighed to God to save
her soul from Satan's fire;
but still farewell she had to wave,
for see, what did transpire:
for just when they the prayer did sound,
she sank and vanished in the ground
that closed itself around her.

Let this example teach each one
who is too arrogant,
and he who willfully goes on
and fights the Lord's command.
For Jesu eye sees everything;
take still more into reckoning,
that He can always find you.

19 · O human soul, keep this in mind,
abandon pride's temptation,
and leave all other sins behind,
they were her ruination.
May this forever keep you free
from sins and pride and vanity,
and you'll inherit Heaven.

49 THE RICH SISTER'S PUNISHMENT
Tape recording from Himmerland by Th. Knudsen, 1961

And once there were two sisters,
one was so rich, so rich,
so poor, so poor was the other,
she hadn't anything.

The poor, the very poor sister
her lonely road does tread
over to her rich sister
to ask for a piece of bread.

"Oh, dearest, dearest sister,
give me a piece of bread;
my seven small children must be fed,
at home I have no bread."

"Oh, no, oh, no, dear sister,
I cannot help at all,
for I shall need the bread myself,
if I should be in want."

5 • And then the poor, poor sister
her lonely road does tread
home to her poor, poor dwelling,
where seven small corpses she found.

When the rich husband came from church
and wanted to cut some bread,
the bread was hard like an iron vise;
the bread was full of blood.

"Oh, dearest, dearest goodwife,
whom did you bread deny?"

"It was my poor, poor sister,
she hadn't any bread."

"Oh, dearest, dearest goodwife,
ask her to be absolved;
her seven small children we must take,
with gold and silver penance make,
if only she will forgive."

There was the rich, rich sister
her lonely road did tread
over to her poor sister
and asked to be absolved.

10 · "O dearest, dearest sister,
if only you will forgive,
your seven small children we shall take,
with gold and silver penance make,
if only you will forgive."

"Oh, dearest, dearest sister,
I can't do that for you:
my seven small children need no bread,
for everyone is dead."

There was the rich, rich sister
her lonely road did tread
home to her wealthy dwelling,
but it was all aflame.

13 · When God removes what's his,
we've nothing to call our own;
but little left there is,
there's nothing that we own.

50 LIE AND TRUTH
Broadside, 1547, including No. 51

Truth was mighty in times gone by,
cherished by all and sundry;
she ruled o'er everyone under the sky,
none put her in a quand'ry.
But Lie has smitten her with her ire,
to hear and see her she doesn't desire
and wants absolutely to oust her.

So to the palace Truth went up
and asked for accomodation.
As soon as she had come to a stop
bewailing her privation,
Lie came riding into the yard
with a host of horsemen as her guard,
with swords that were drawn and ready.

Lie they supported in noble chiffon
with honor and great admiration;
Truth she heard it at once and anon,
and she felt deep desolation.
Truth she hurried out of the place,
for being saved she thanked God's grace,
her life it almost had cost her.

Truth she sped to the country town,
where town asylum she courted;
but when that to Lie became known,
she wanted that she should be thwarted.
Lie sent the mayors and councils a bill,
demanding that Truth at once they kill,
that she shouldn't linger with them.

5 • Then about midnight Truth took flight
to foil the townsmen's ruses,
because they labored with all their might
to harm her with stealth and abuses.
Thus she fled to the peasant's cot,
to stay a couple of years she thought,
that Lie no more would find her.

Lie wrote letters to every court
that Truth should be escorted
in heavy chains up to the fort,
and they would be rewarded;
or else the peasant she would infest
with daily evil and woe and pest,
and nothing would flourish for him.

Truth had no place on Earth to stay
where she'd find peace and quiet;
so to the conclave she steered her way
to further her mission by it.
Bishops and prelates rejected her plea,
because she denounced their finery
which they had no right to brandish.

Truth had then to the abbey gone,
at the bishops she couldn't tarry;
she put a lowly cassock on,
its meekness she meant to carry.
Truth asked the monks to fight 'gainst Lie,
that she with them for a while might stay,
that might be a boon for the abbey.

"Truth, you are only a fugitive,
nobody holds you dear;
thus in the abbey you cannot live,
we will not fight for you here.

Now we serve Lie with loyalty,
to us you can only harmful be,"
so everybody told her.

10 · "Lie is rich and stays with us,
nobody in salvation
can be found who makes less fuss
and gives us more elation.
Lie she builds quite heavy walls,
and no labor us befalls
but she will coax us to it.

Truth, you are both hungry and frail,
with meager grub without flavor,
you are welcome at our jail,
and that is what you shall savor."
Truth is now chained to the prison bunk,
and Lie is patron saint of the monk
who wants to kill Truth by starvation.

If only Truth had friends or folk
to speak in favor of her
and ask them their anger to revoke
and leave to go allow her.
May God in Heaven come to her aid,
the monks have done her a wrong so great,
for she is, indeed, quite blameless.

Truth is presently in a plight,
that's felt by each and every;
Satan is working day and night
to strengthen Lie by deviltry.
Whenever Truth can speak again,
you better, Lie, start running then,
you know what that will cost you.

14 · 'Tis only a very few who know,
that Truth her chains has broken;
they praise the Lord, both high and low,
in words that are felt, not just spoken.
The Papists she hurts so grievously,
because she lays bare their perfidy
which gave them all their power.

51 THE CASSOCK
Broadside, 1547, including No. 50

Oh, cassock, you're made by the evil ghost,
for thousands of souls by you are lost,
who trusted you to the very last
instead of God and His mercy so vast.

Oh, cassock, you are a trap of Hell,
through you so many Christians fell
by the false indulgence you carried around;
in you the greatest rogue is found.

Oh, cassock, just look around and stop,
for our best things you have eaten up;
the needy widow, the orphan child
you robbed like the beasts so fierce and wild.

Oh, cassock, why the cardinal's hat
you bought from the pope in Rome – for what?
For eighteen thousand guilders good,
though they were poor people's food.

5 · Oh, cassock, you are so great a plague,
for the poor peasant sorrow and ache;
you rob him both of his silver and gold
with the indulgences that you hold.

Oh, cassock, your knavery now lies bare,
God's word you treated like market ware;
gold ring, buckle and silver belt
often into your possession fell.

Oh, cassock, your pope they hanged in a noose,
the monks still scurry, free and loose;
they carry his brand for all to see;
oh, cassock, that must never be.

Oh, cassock, you are all evil's skin,
for you made use of shame and sin;
the word of God you won't listen to,
but whoring and murder you often do.

9 •Oh, cassock, bethink you shall die, you too,
and save yourself from Hell and its woe;
and when you stand before God's throne,
no pope can bring you help from Rome. *Amen.*

52 MAY SONG

Tape recording from Himmerland by Th. Knudsen, 1959

Good day, my honest man, good day
– *May, you're welcome* –
and may we sing for you today?
– *Be happy for such a sweet summer.*

Summer is heading our way,
winter comes some other day.

Summer we have in our poke,
winter rests in Halkier bog.

We've a maypole, high and wide,
was raised on the eve of Whitsuntide.

5 · We dug through sand, and we dug through clay,
– *May, you're welcome* –
for fifteen years it's bound to stay.
– *Be happy for such a sweet summer.*

We raised the maypole so very high
that all can see it in the sky.

We raised it with permission good,
for it has grown in our master's wood.

Our master is a decent sport,
he pours us drinks from his mug and pot.

Our mistress is a pleasant wife,
she gives us pennies, twenty five.

10 · His hired man and hired maid,
they give us pennies, seven, eight.

Our music maker you mustn't forget,
you give him pennies for pic and fret.

Our Cinderella is quite a wag,
you give him both for his sack and bag.

Oh, thanks, oh, thanks, you friendly host,
for all the money we thank you most.

Yes, you shall have so many thanks,
as heaven is bestrewn with stars.

15 · Now we shall go away from here
and wish you all a happy year.

Good-bye, ye women, good-bye, ye men,
this year we shan't come back again.

17 · And now we doff our hats so light
– *May, you're welcome* –
and wish you all a quiet night.
– *Be happy for such a sweet summer.*

This was the way they sang, when they were received well. If they did not get anything, the end of the ditty was hardly as nice. Then it ran:

But he who's rich, but nothing gives,
the devil plague him while he lives.

19 · And he who sleeps and won't arise,
– *May, you're welcome* –
may he be eaten by fleas and lice.
– *Be happy for such a sweet summer.*

9 · ROMANCES

53 THE TWO ROYAL CHILDREN
Recording from Harboöre by Karen Thuborg

Two noble children of royal birth
they pledged each other their troth;
to live together they wanted,
one roof to shelter them both.

"But how shall I come over to thee,
across the white-topped wave?
There are so many billows blue
that can become my grave."

"Thou must dive in on your chest so white
and swim across to me;
and I shall light my lanterns nine,
and they shall shine for thee."

But outside stood a devilish maid
and heard the words they spoke;
she doused the light of the lanterns nine
that burned for the royal boy.

5 · Inside sat all the convent maidens
and worked with golden thread;
one of them was his sweetheart dear,
tears on her cheek she shed.

In she went to her mother dear
\- - - - -
and asked for leave that she might go
down to the roaring sea.

"All by thyself thou mustn't go
down to the roaring sea.
Awaken thou must thy younger brother
and he shall follow thee."

"If I awaken my younger brother,
ever thoughtless before,
he always shoots the little birds
that fly along the shore."

"All by thyself thou mustn't go
down to the roaring sea.
Awaken thou must thy younger sister,
and she shall follow thee."

10 • "If I awaken my younger sister,
ever thoughtless before,
then she'll pick all the little flowers
that grow along the shore."

All by herself the maiden went
down to the roaring sea;
there she was met by a fisherman
who had just landed his skiff.

"Oh, listen, my good fisherman,
if thou dost fish for meed,
then fish me up the royal boy
who drowned in our sea."

"Yes, I have fished throughout the night,
caught nothing while afloat,

but for a little royal boy,
lies in the stern of my boat."

Then she drew from her finger a ring,
it was of the purest gold:
"This ring is for thyself as meed,
if you will trade with me."

15 • She lifted up the royal boy
and sealed his mouth with a kiss.
Together they took the sorry road
down in the deep abyss.

54 DANYSER ("TANNHÄUSER")
Broadside, 1580

A lovely old song about a knight by name of Danyser
who stayed in Lady Venus' mountain,
in which we shall see, what evil licentiousness brings on,
for such blind and forbidden love ends always in sorrow.

Right now I shall begin to sing
of Danyser the knight
and Lady Venus and the things
they did in joy and delight.

Danyser was so bold a knight
with wondrous things to face,
he yearned for the mountain with all his might,
for Venus and all her maids.

And when a year had come to an end,
his sins made him grieve and rue;
to Lady Venus he therefore went
and said: "I want leave of you."

"Sir Danyser, we hold you dear;
if that is in your heart,
think of the oath you swore right here,
never with us to part."

5 · "My Lady Venus, I answer you Nay!
That I shall loudly deny;
I do not believe in what you say,
and now let me greet you good-bye."

"Sir Danyser, don't talk that way,
among us you must live;
you choose one of my maids, you may,
she's mine, for me to give."

If I should change my plans instead
of what I now desire,
to Hell I surely would be led
and to the eternal fire."

"You talk about Hell to where you are led,
you know not, if it is right;
but just you think of my mouth so red,
that's laughing both day and night."

"What kind of help is your mouth to me
when I in the fire must quake?
Oh, gracious lady, set me free
for every maiden's sake."

10 · "We shan't permit you to go away,
Danyser, as you contrive;
stay with us and be a knight so gay,
enjoy your youthful life."

"My life is too straight wherever I turn,
and it must come to an end;
confession and penance, for that I yearn,
forever I shall repent."

"Danyser, Danyser, don't talk that way,
for don't you see, it's in vain?
Let us go into my chamber gay,
with us you shall remain."

"You talk to me of your chamber gay,
your heart is full of evil;
I see it in your eyes so grey,
you are a woman devil."

"Danyser, Danyser, don't scold us that way,
why do you talk in that vein?
For such behavior I'd make you pay,
should you with us remain."

15 · "Venus, it shan't be otherwise,
to you I won't give in.
Help me, Lord in Paradise,
against this woman of sin."

"Danyser, we shall you with furlough provide
and show you the road that is best;
and you shall, wherever you may ride,
sing our praise, we request."

At once he left the mountain,
alive and stout at heart:
"Now help me, Christ in Paradise,
do not from me depart.

I want to go to Rome to see,
if I shall be helped by it,
whether pope Urban can succor me
and all my sins remit." –

"O Holy Father, pope so great,
my sins I repent and rue
that I 'gainst God did perpetrate,
them shall I confess to you.

20 · For a year in sin's and error's ruse
with Venus I let me ensnare;
woe and my sins me now accuse,
in confession I lay them bare."

The pope he had a staff in his hand
and planted it in the ground:
"Whenever this staff a-blooming stands,
forgiveness you shall have found."

Danyser told the town good-bye
with sorrow and also great pain:
"Oh, help me, Holy Christ on high,
God comfort each sorrowful swain.

Cursed be the pope for this awful tort
that sends me to Hell and its pain;
a soul they're taking from the Lord
that might with him remain."

And when he to the mountain did go,
he looked around him and sighed:
"God bless the sun and the moon also."
And into the mountain he hied.

25 · Into the mountain entered he,
they welcomed him heartily there:
"Tell us, Danyser, immediately,
tell us, how did you fare?"

"I could have sworn that it nowise
would ever happen to me;
I pray to Christ in Paradise
that still I saved may be."

It happened after the second day
the staff began to look green;
ere night it stood with flowers and leaves,
fairer than ever seen.

The pope sent word both East and West:
"Danyser, come back without fail;
from sin and evil you are wrest
by Christ, to your avail."

The pope sank into sadness and rue
and prayed at every mass
that God let Danyser's wish come true,
forgive him his trespass.

30 · Oh, Venus, Venus, how you are blind,
how many a man have you spoiled,
that he loses both his heart and mind,
by ugly errors soiled.

31 · He who will sin against God's grace
is paid with eternal despair;
thus put yourself in Danyser's place,
watch out for sin and take care.

55 COBBLER AND NOBLEMAN
Ida Giöe's Manuscript, about 1630

Oh, harken my lords, both small and great,
to what I shall in my song narrate,
it's worth to listen to:
of a cobbler and a nobleman,
you'll see what they shall do.

The cobbler had a pretty wife
– so many, alas, you find in life –
the stars could almost envy her;
the nobleman couldn't but think of her
and often wanted to see her.

The nobleman he went in and out,
he always wanted to be about
with the wife in the cobbler's house;
he didn't come for the cobbler's sake,
but for the cobbler's spouse.

The cobbler thought deep down in his heart:
"The squire is good and takes my part
(he's simple as can be)
for if he needs either boots or shoes
then he comes always to me."

5 • The squire came oft to the cobbler's house
for a talk and a couple of bottles' carouse
and a joke and a laugh to boot;
the woman he treated with winks and pats;
the journeyman understood.

The lad turned it over in his mind:
"How much of this joking can you find
without any woe or strife?
How can there be so much faithlessness
in the wily heart of a wife?"

At last the journeyman told his boss:
"I think that you are due for a loss,
this is no cause for laughter.
This nobleman doesn't come for naught,
'tis your wife he is running after."

The cobbler got a shock so great
and asked the lad both early and late:
"What is it all about?
I beg you, give me your advice,
how shall I best find out?"

"Collect your money," said the lad,
"and tell them that your need is bad,
you must make haste and hie
yourself to market right away,
for leather you must buy.

10 · And then you hide yourself in the house
and keep as quiet as a mouse
and see what will occur;
for by your pious wife you will
be made a fool, I swear."

The cobbler did as told by the lad,
and hidden himself in the house he had;
she started a merry do:
she thought her husband was far away,
the nobleman thought so, too.

When evening came and there was no trace
of daylight, he went to the cobbler's place
as fast as he could be;
the woman who was all prepared
received him graciously.

They went to bed as they wanted to,
and there was a merry and happy ado;
short was the fun to be:
The cobbler outside the bedroom stood,
an angry man was he.

And soon their passion they had spent,
into the room the cobbler went,
they were asleep, he found;
he mulled it over in his mind
what punishment would be sound.

15 • "To kill him doesn't help, I say,
so I will find a better way."
See, what he did to them both:
it sounds just like a liar's tale,
for he took off his clothes.

Beside the bed lay the nobleman's
beautiful cloak, his coat and pants;
he crouched and put them on,
the sword he fastened at his side
and out of the house he did run.

And on the nobleman's door he knocked,
that by the page was fast unlocked;
the boy he turned the handle
and said: "Where have you been so long?
Please, let me light a candle."

"No, let it be, my boy," he said.
"Despite the dark I'll find the bed;
be careful how you fare,
so that my wife will not awake,
for that I wouldn't care."

The lady thought it was heaven sent:
"How nice that my husband is diligent!"
and she was greatly impressed
because the knight was so passionate –
the cobbler did his best.

20 · The lady said: "My dearest knight,
have all your fun, all your delight,
and that I shall repay;
I'll make a supper of the best,
it seldom comes your way."

When through the window dawn did peep,
the lady she was fast asleep,
the cobbler looked around;
and so the squire's Sunday clothes
he in the cupboard found.

He put them on with greatest speed
and then he went into the street,
and he stuck out his chest;
his clothes they were so beautiful,
velvet and silk of the best.

The nobleman came also to life,
lying beside the cobbler's wife
without his clothes in sight;
for him, quite naked, the cobbler's clothes
would have to do in his plight.

Without his clothing he became
filled in his heart with the greatest shame
and said: "'Tis the woman's fault;
and I must think of another way,
if to fornicate I feel called."

25 · And he went home the shortest way,
but was betaken with great dismay
when the cobbler he saw in the square;
he had the cobbler's clothing on,
while the cobbler his did wear.

"Where are you going, tell me, come on?"
The cobbler said: "Where you just came from,
to my house, that is my aim;
and where now your feet are taking you
is the place, from where I came."

"How comes that it is my clothes you wear?"
he asked, and the cobbler did declare
with full equanimity:
"'Cause everything is turned upside down,
and so I am rich, you see."

They'd given each other poke and pat,
and each of them got tit for tat,
they had to laugh at each other.
But many who want to fornicate
should think before they bother.

Thus counsel I you, both great and small,
for fornication you mustn't fall,
for Jesu mercy you pray,
that, like the nobleman, you not
shall end in shame and dismay.

30 • We read a lot of woman's snare,
how Samson with Delilah did fare,
intent on fornication.
And so I counsel every man,
beware of such damnation.

31 • Although this song I did translate,
the good I didn't want to berate,
but I intended to warn,
that those who delve in vice and sin
shall always be forlorn.

10 · STORIES ABOUT LOVE

56 THE LOST FALCON

Svaning's Manuscript I, about 1580

One day I went for a pleasure ride
in a wood so green and hilly,
and there I saw two roses
and the most beautiful lily;
the birds were singing with lovely thrill,
each with a voice of her own;
it made my heart so still.

And I rode down from a hilltop
where I saw a brooklet run;
beside it I found a maiden,
the loveliest under the sun.
I spoke to her with joy in my heart,
she answered graciously, but with a sigh,
and then she started to cry.

Immediately I got off my horse,
and I walked up to her:
"I beg you to tell me, lovely maid,
o'er whom you are so upset?"
"By nobody am I upset,
but I have lost a precious thing,
there is no cure for it."

"Please, tell me then, my lovely maid,
tell me, what is your loss?"

"Young sir, that I would gladly do,
if comfort it would cause.
Once I did tame a falcon fine,
but now the falcon has flown away,
wherefore I sorrow and pine."

5 · "Lend me your ear, my lovely maid,
my counsel surpasses the rest:
you put your reliance in our Lord,
he manages for the best.
Grief for the falcon you need not endure,
if you will give your love to one
much finer than him before."

"The falcon he is so dear to my heart,
that I cannot give him up;
whenever I was together with him
it made my sorrow stop.
Thus I must sorrow constantly,
with longing and grief in heart and mind,
great woe is in store for me."

"Lend me your ear, my lovely maid,
and give your heart to me,
as long as the falcon deserted you
whom you praise so excessively.
And I shall never make you cry,
but I shall honor and love you
until the day I die."

8 · The falcon flies and has lost his way,
nobody's fault but his own;
his happiness did he forfeit himself,
the grief by himself was sown;
his heart shall never feel joy's caress,
thus he must grieve himself to death –
that is the pay for all faithlessness. *Amen.*

57 WATCHMAN'S SONG
The Heart Book, 1553–55

The winter night is cold and long,
that I must highly rue;
how can I find my sweetheart dear
with honor and virtue true?
I wandered around the castle with woe,
and I was really all in;
I begged the watchman with all my heart:
"Help me that I may win.

Good watchman, understand my plea,
and what I have to say;
for any good advice you have,
handsomely I shall pay.
I shall be ready with my reward
for counsel, honest and fit,
and I shall make you rich enough
that you can afford to quit."

The watchman vanishes secretly
and knocks at the door with zest:
"Wake up, wake up, my pretty maid,
I bring you happiness.
You promise me by hand and mouth
that me you won't betray:
somebody stands outside the gate,
you make him happy and gay."

"Be silent, watchman, don't talk that way,
and heed what you are saying;
the lad I love with all my heart,
for him I am pining and praying,
he is so far, so far away,
thus I know better, you see.
O watchman, if you tell the truth,
rewarded you shall be."

5 · The watchman then began to scold
with anger in his eye:
"I've served you for a long, long time
and never told you a lie.
You let me know upon your creed,
if you'll keep faith at all;
I'll help the guest who trusts me best
across both grating and wall."

At the same moment he opened up
the door to ecstasy,
the virtue of love became their guest,
and sorrow was made to flee.
Then followed a talk in secrecy
that a poet could never express,
because they were together again
in honor and happiness.

The watchman began to sing a song,
it sounded far and wide:
"Wherever there is an unwelcome guest,
he fears the end of the night;
he uses both common sense and wit,
of help it will never be,
if he stays on, my property
and life is in jeopardy."

The maiden in her lover's arms
she heaved a woeful sigh,
her rosy cheeks became so pale,
have pity, God on high.
"Good watchman, why do you sadden me,
what use can it be to you?
We came together not long ago,
the night isn't halfway through."

9 · The maiden opened the window up,
and she was heavy-hearted;
she saw the shining morning star,
and all her joy departed.
"I will commit you to God, my dear,
the day shines far and near,
I will commit you to Jesus Christ,
for He can bring us cheer."

58 THE THREE NOBLEMEN
Recording from Harboöre by Karen Thuborg

Fair maiden she stands on highest hill
and looks at the roaring sea;
she saw then a ship come sailing towards shore
in which three noblemen sat.

The youngest of them went up the hill
to ask for the maiden's hand.
He wished to betroth the maiden fair,
although he was so young.

And then he drew out of his pocket
a ring of the reddest gold
and put it on the maiden's hand:
"'Tis the bond of faithfulness.

I shall now set out on a journey
that'll last for seven years;
but then I shall surely come home again
to you, my little dear."

5 · When the seven years journey was over,
the youth came home at last;
his father greeted him at the door:
"Welcome, welcome, my son.

You are too late by an hour,
for today your sweetheart was wed."
"And who shall then be my dearest one?
Nobody knows but God."

Whereafter he entered his chamber
to comb and curl his hair,
and then he saddled his steed so grey
and rode to the house of the bride.

The banquet hall he entered
and took the bride by her hand:
and while they then were dancing around,
her rosy cheeks turned pale.

"Why are your cheeks so sallow
when they were red before?"
"Because false tongues have lied to me
and told me you were no more."

10 · "Alas, have false tongues lied to you
and told you I was no more,
it'll only be an hour
before you shall see my blood."

Whereafter he entered his chamber
and bolted the chamber door
and seated himself on his golden chair
and then wrote letters three.

And when the letters were written
and the hour at last had passed,
he rose and drew his shiny bayonet
and buried it in his heart.

And when the blood was running
and streaming out of his veins,

he opened the door he had locked before:
"Come, little dear, and see!"

"God save me, unhappy maiden,
and tell me what I shall do.
For one is on the brink of the grave,
the other is drowning in his blood."

15 · Fair maiden she stands on highest hill
and looks at the roaring sea;
then she spread out her golden hair,
jumped into the waves so blue.

59 THE RE-UNION
Recording by Selma Nielsen

A starlit evening I walked around
in Friendship's Park, at the green;
I stopped in wonder when flowers I found
as pretty as ever seen.

While thus I wandered around and thought
of Heaven's great benefaction
and wonders created by the Lord
for everyone's station and action.

I suddenly heard, not far remote,
a voice with enravishing timbre;
the song came out of a lovely throat
that I shall always remember.

I walked towards the voice, and then I saw
a maid on the grass at a tree;
she looked so sorrowful where she sat
'mongst flowers so pretty to see.

5 · Without any guile I did ascend
and said to the maid: "My dear,
would you allow me to be your friend?
It seems that you are my peer."

She answered with tears in utter dismay:
"Kind sir, that I cannot do.
Please, do as I ask you and go away
and leave me alone to my woe."

I pondered a moment with pounding heart
and looked at the maid so sad:
When she insisted to sorrow alone,
what was it that was so bad?

"Please, have you a father or mother here
or kinfolks to come to your aid;
or have you a lover whom you hold dear?
Please, tell me about it, dear maid."

Her color changed to a deadly white:
"Oh, kindhearted sir," she said,
the while she looked towards heaven and sighed,
"then hear why I hang my head.

10 · My father he drowned in the stormy sea,
of sorrow my mother did die;
and thus in loneliness I must be,
and cry by myself must I.

I had a brother who disappeared,
he sailed the ocean blue;
for seven long years I haven't heard
from him, no letter came through.

A lover I had who vanished also,
his father had a cold heart;
to foreign countries he forced him to go
to keep us forever apart."

"Who was the lover that wasn't true?
I beg you to answer me straight.
And what was his station? I pray that you
will tell me at once, dear maid."

"His father's station and name was Earl John,
and he himself was called Thor;
it's three years ago I saw the son,
God knows if we meet evermore."

15 · I stood for a moment and pondered her fate,
my blood ran a furious race.
"Oh, beautiful Mary, oh, that it is you!
Come into your Thor's embrace."

16 · The maiden became so happy indeed,
Thor was in a joyful whirl,
because he now saw his dream succeed
and found his beloved girl.

11 · THE WOMAN WORSHIPPED

60 PER RÆV LILLE'S LOVE SONG
Theological Miscellany, about 1470–80

The glorious rays of love I praise
with song and joy sublime;
a flower whose name I won't pronounce
I'll bless in the selfsame rhyme.
She has both beauty and purity,
is wise, without any treachery
and true without devilment;
like all the stars come next to the sun,
so are all women, yes, every-one
to her, whom I speak anent.
Oh, yes, Oh, yes
if only for me she would send.

Be it only my boon the lovely bloom
that chains my heart to see,
I wouldn't know of any woe,
if she would speak to me,
she whom I love above everything;
if all the world's women stood in a ring,
the prettiest crowd of all,
then you would find her peer nowhere
'mongst ladies and maidens ever so fair,
wherever you look or call.
Oh, yes, Oh, yes
Christ save her against a fall.

A lily like no other in the world,
was ever so dear to me,
and she will always be in my heart
wherever she may be.
The Lord in Heaven must surely know
that I am like dead, for I sorrow so,
both in my heart and mind.
The woe that will forever smart
she has impressed into my heart;
may still I gladness find!
Oh, yes, Oh, yes
let still the lily be mine.

But now I feel it in my soul
that she will break with me.
I wish that Christ who masters all,
will make her plans succeed.
I honestly believe that she
the loveliest woman will ever be,
Christ grant her to find her peer.
The lily wants that we shall part,
and I am just an unhappy heart
that couldn't keep her near.
Oh, yes, Oh, yes
what do you want, my dear?

5 · Now I shall change my mood again,
as we together can't be;
I'll etch the lily deep in my heart
from now to eternity;
and there her picture shall always be furled,
e'en if she were at the end of the world
and I at the holy grave.
And I am ready to do her will,
yes, creep on my knees 'cross field and hill,
if she the order gave.
Oh, yes, Oh, yes
for her I shall always crave.

61 HIS SWEETHEART'S DEATH
Langebek's Quarto Manuscript, about 1571

The time when everything went my way,
I had both joy and fair weather;
I had me then a maiden betrothed,
we had great joy together.
– *I'm happy with all my heart.*

And yet she isn't uncommonly fair,
you may well find her match;
but her mien and manners they suit her well,
so say both poor and rich.
– *I'm happy with all my heart.*

And while she is not uncommonly rich
in worldly goods and ways,
to her father and mother obedient she is,
theirs to teach and raise.
– *I'm happy with all my heart.*

And came the time I went abroad,
it was with sorrow so great.
And it was only a short time after
she was in her coffin laid.
– *I sorrow with all my heart.*

5 • Oh, world, oh, world, how strange you are,
bemoan it we do not dare;
you took my sweetheart away from me
for whom I always did care.
– *I sorrow with all my heart.*

Now I will put my trust in God,
all in His care I'll place.
Then He takes away my sorrow and woe,
also the long, long days.
– *I sorrow with all my heart.*

7 · Now we shall lie in the earth together
and both have peace and rest,
until we shall arise again
for the heavenly Master to bless.
– *I sorrow with all my heart.*

62 A SAD COMPLAINT OF SEPARATION
Broadside, 1648

Qveremonia Venerea.
That is:
A sad plaint over his sweetheart's
sudden departure and separation.

Parting, oh, parting, why are you so hard,
why do you touch me so?
You torture me more than I can stand,
I to my grave must go.
Oh, could we just walk once more and talk,
my heart's ever dearest friend.

You offer me your hand so white,
I give my hand to you;
God set it right that side by side
we walk and talk anew
in woody dell that suits you well,
my heart's ever dearest friend.

You know it is pain and sorrow so great
when two have each other dear
and must from each other separate
and cannot tarry near;
still more it smarts the lonely hearts,
my heart's ever dearest friend.

Longing has taken hold of me
with great tristfulness,
that I to none but you, my sweet,
my feelings can address.
You bring me ease and my heart's release,
my heart's ever dearest friend.

5 · Under the sky's bright firmament
never did I see
anybody in my ken
more beloved by me
than you, my dearest, divinest and fairest,
my heart's ever dearest friend.

The sun enraptures me frequently
with its wonderful shine;
you do the same, my darling, to me
with that nearness of thine.
My joy and my bliss, my golden miss,
my heart's ever dearest friend.

Alas, where dwells your noble form,
beautiful to behold,
enchanting to me and bringing me balm
always manifold,
like wonderful flowers in groves and in bowers,
my heart's ever dearest friend.

Away now is the joy of my eyes
and my great delight.
Woe and sorrow have crossed my way,
solace is not in sight,
until I can glance at your countenance,
my heart's ever dearest friend.

My little swan, oh, where did you fly
over the salty sea?
'Neath your soft wing why couldn't you try
to bring and shelter me?
That I bewail through life without fail,
my heart's ever dearest friend.

10 · Alas, where are now your friendly mind
and your words so wise,
your mouth so rosy, your cheek so kind
and your gentle eyes?
You alone, the most precious stone,
my heart's ever dearest friend.

Just as the dove on snow-white beach
who has lost her mate
sorrows as he is no more in reach,
that is also my fate;
to long and wizen is like a prison,
my heart's ever dearest friend.

Awake or asleep, by day or night,
I see you appear,
and in my dreams with joy and delight
I feel you are near.
But when I awake from this I miss
my heart's ever dearest friend.

Virtuous, warm, yes, wonderful, fine
you appear to me,
gentle and mild, untouched and divine
you I often see.
My heart is delighted, though it is blighted,
my heart's ever dearest friend.

My joy and pleasure have come to an end
for this love of mine;
I know not where to turn, anent
you again to find.
You've torn my heart painfully apart,
my heart's ever dearest friend.

15 • It's hard to part and say good-night
to our parents dear,
sister and brother, family and kin;
but it does appear
ever so hard from her to depart,
my heart's ever dearest friend.

As a lonely bird will pine and fret
in the maple tree,
because he suffered the loss of his mate,
so it goes with me.
She has left me and has bereft me
my heart's ever dearest friend.

I have no peace of mind and soul,
no refuge at all,
before I again your hand can hold
and your fingers small,
when I rejoice at hearing your voice,
my heart's ever dearest friend.

Princes and kings, when face to face,
hug with great display;
but, my darling, I shall embrace
in Tobias' way,
with warmest greeting and kisses befitting,
my heart's ever dearest friend.

My darling, farewell, my darling, adieu,
good-bye, pretty bloom.
Let us hope that we meet anew
and be happy soon;
'mongst friends let it be in decency,
my heart's ever dearest friend.

20 · May Raphael, the archangel, lead you well
on your path through life;
may you be saved by Emmanuel
from injury and strife.
In prayer, genuflected, I never neglected
my heart's ever dearest friend.

21 · My darling, know, that I have no doubt
you'll remember me
with a yearning that will stretch out
into eternity.
Don't forget as I won't forget,
my heart's ever dearest friend.

63 THE BEAUTIFUL TREE
Langebek's Quarto Manuscript, about 1575

I know where I can find a tree
that's raised in faith and duty,
and it shall be my sweetheart dear,
developed in all its beauty.
If she would deign to change her mind
and love me more than all,
I promise on the Holy Book
my troth would never pall.

The tree is guarded carefully
by turrets and walls so wide;
there sing skylark and nightingale,
my sweetheart sleeps inside;
and nothing is a-thriving in there
but rose and carnation red;
when I pine for my ever dear,
I wish that I were dead.

There is no one in this world
who can deny me this tree;
it leans with both its branches and roots
with all its might towards me.
And who shall ever stop me,
for she is so dear to me;
for more than anything in this world
my only joy is she.

The slanderer with his evil tongue
he wants to touch the flower;
he shall not do it, for I shall fight
against him with all my power.
Sooner shall he from heartbreak die
than he shall have his way;
for none shall ever keep us apart
in all our living days.

5 · May Jesus Christ in Paradise
and all his angels there
protect her well, my ever-sweet,
wherever she may fare;
whether here or abroad,
now or all along,
O Lord, protect my ever-sweet
from any evil tongue.

64 A HEART SO TRUE

The Heart Book, 1553–55, compare No. 79

To all intent, a heart so true
for you shall always be fain;
and it is only caused by you
that I am your loving swain.
'Tis easy to tell
I love you well,
by yearning I almost kill myself,
when we apart remain.

By grace that you have given me
a chain between us is spun.
Now comes the traducer with perfidy
and thinks that he has won.
Don't heed, I pray,
his deceitful way,
resist him stoutly and answer Nay,
and let me feel your troth.

You promised by hand and by mouth before
all others you would forgo,
that you would love me for evermore;
now you don't want it so.
But one who chose
to reason, knows
it doesn't matter how it goes,
I'll never be false to you.

4 · You chill me with inconstancy,
if I'm cast off like this;
as if you have never known of me,
me you will now dismiss.
My heart's great woe
and life's hardship, too,
make day and night so slow, so slow;
who'll bring me happiness?

65 ROSINA
Langebek's Quarto Manuscript, before 1563

"Rosina, where were you so fair
during the time of King Paris,
when he the gold-apple had in his care
to give to the ever fairest?
Believe me, I pray,
if Paris could lay
his eyes on your form and feature,
proud Venus the apple wouldn't have got,
the prize had been yours, dear creature.

And if Vergilius had known you while
for Helen of Troy, whose beauty
surpassed all others, he used his style,
he would have thought it his duty
to lavish on you
a picture still greater
of heavenly beauty and dazzle;
thus I have taken in you more pleasure,
and I shall be your vassal."

3 · "O youth, this shall be your meed for all
your kindness and warm ovation:
in all your need my mouth so red
shall be your consolation,
as mister Ywain
from Luneta had
with greatest praise and homage;
to love you better than anyone else
on Earth I verily promise."

66 HAPPINESS IN LOVE
Jens Bille's Manuscript, 1555–59

The flowers grow, and the sun it shines,
the Earth is fully at ease;
over the hills and vales the dew
drifts from the sky in a breeze.

So it goes with a human heart
when it has ease and relief;
if it meets its dearest friend,
they laugh away their grief.

She who has a faithful friend
and never more than one,
she loves him well and stands by him,
their love will keep on and on.

I'm thinking of her beneath the bush
that is with roses bestowed;
and off that bush I'll pick me one,
my one and only beloved.

5 • She who loves more men than one
is only a Jezebel;
and if she has more friends than me,
it is against my will.

He who harbors a secret sorrow
and doesn't bruit it about
before he meets his dearest friend,
on his own he wants to make out.

May God give my sweetheart as many good nights
as heaven is lit by the stars and their lights;
may God give my sweetheart as many good years
as the maple has leaves and the doe has hairs.

8 • I haven't more to sing about friends,
think of it I always do;
I love that friend who holds me dear,
and fancy that so can you.

67 ERIK LANGE TO SOPHIE BRAHE
Queen Sofia's Manuscript, 1584

Abandon, my soul, your lofty desire,
abandon your glorious hunger,
let be the apple you can't acquire,
and tire yourself no longer.
– *Destiny never changes.*

Futile your hope and your valiant mood,
so small is the strength of thine;
abandon the mood you think is good,
free me from the chains of mine.

Why feed the flame and keep on and on,
by it you may be molested,
when it ignites the glowing sun
and cannot be arrested.

You woeful creature, you clod of earth
who always see darkness before you;
you are not worthy to feel the joy
that the sun should be shining o'er you.

5 • Why do you say that it's in vain
what still may be nurtured on?
Silent hope can accomplish much
and change what couldn't be done.

Never the apple so high on bough
which ripens by sun and shower,
that some time will fall to the ground below,
may God speed up the hour.
– *Destiny never changes.*

The falcon may sit so high on the wall,
the beasts be as free as ever,
even they have to fear for a fall,
if the hunter's planning be clever.

My strength is far greater than you know,
this I invisibly hide;
I'm not alone: wherever I go
great power is at my side.

A joyful constraint is the jail of your choice,
light the load you love to have drawn;
in tears that end in song you rejoice,
short the night with a lovely dawn.

10 · Why shouldn't I make the fire go on
that both ignites and smothers?
It's quenched by the dew which burns in the sun,
and will not be changed by others.

Why should I fear for the distress
that still keeps me alive?
Short is the pain which ends in death
and that can still revive.

The Earth has beasts and the river fish,
they're spread so far around;
the birds they soar in the air so fresh,
so high over valley and mount.

Thus it is possible that there may
be creatures alive in the fire,
wherein they both can rejoice and play,
all to their heart's desire.
– *Destiny never changes.*

Then shine, O sun, with all your glow,
burn him who wants to burn;
you may desire to melt like snow
the hopes that ardently yearn.

15 · In all the world there is nobody
who'd know these hopes in my mind
but you alone, if you just cared,
the others are far behind.

But shadows of your magnificence,
they follow your clarity;
they are against your eminence
like weeds 'gainst a linden tree.

17 · Be done, my song, I have managed well
the thoughts you gave me to handle.
A hint is enough for such as can tell,
wise jesting is gravity's mantle.
– *Destiny never changes.*

12 · THE WOMAN LONGING

68 SOPHIE BRAHE TO ERIK LANGE
Ida Giöe's Manuscript, about 1630

Pray, harken, I beseech you,
and I shall sing a song
about my love and beloved
who aims to do me wrong.
– *My ever dearest, do never forget me.*

One thing is certain, my love for him
out of my heart has sprung;
I do not heed either friend or kin
and never a wagging tongue.

You shall not know from this, how deep
my love is, I won't let you;
but you shall never see the day
on which I can forget you.

I love you in all honesty
and with a heart that's true;
how often haven't I sorrowed and pined
for longing and yearning for you.

5 · But sooner would I die for you
– my life I'm ready to offer –
than feel, my dearest, beloved friend,
that you the least should suffer.

By yearning and by deepest love
my heart has long been melted,
I cannot doubt, my ever-dear,
that you yourself have felt it.
– *My ever dearest, do never forget me.*

O love of mine, how strange you are,
o'er you I'm woebegone;
for her who loves you best of all
it's easiest for you to shun.

You do not want to be sated
either with mead or wine;
for we have talked together,
your heart beats just like mine.

And since I always loved but you
with all my mind and might,
your heart has always yearned for me,
you told me to my delight.

10 • 'Mongst all the people who live in the world
and on the Earth may dwell,
there never lives in the wide, wide world
another I love so well.

I know you full well, my dearest love,
your heart belongs to me;
I felt it ever so often when
with friends you didn't agree.

Now they have counseled you here and there,
from early until late,
and now you find yourself some place
where you would celebrate.

And like the hunter who rides in the bush,
up to the beasts from behind:
then he will often find the one
he didn't intend to find.
– *My ever dearest, do never forget me.*

He wants to shoot the bird who has
a golden egg in her nest;
but he may easily miss his goal
and hit a Robin Readbreast.

15 · Yes, you have followed your friends' advice
and looked for riches and lands;
but still you haven't obtained a thing
but play and music bands.

The trumpet, the organ, the lyre and lute
won't last, come another day;
beware of them, my dearest friend,
they want to lead you astray.

Then watch yourself, my dearest friend,
they want to lead you astray;
oh, Lord, it would sadden me most of all,
if you should suffer dismay.

What I have told you all is true,
rely on it, I pray you;
but you shall never see the day,
my dear, when I'll betray you.

Before you let me understand,
your love for me was so deep,
and when we talked together,
the two of us did weep.

20 • Then separation came afterwards,
was caused by riches and gold,
though if it's true what I have heard,
but little of it you hold.
– *My ever dearest, do never forget me.*

They promised you thousands that she would
bring home with her to you;
but when you are taking the maiden home,
much less will have to do.

If never you got the fortune so great
that they held up for your eyes,
I thank my God for my friends and kin,
from them I can get advice.

I trust you, my dear, beloved friend,
desert me you never will;
you know full well, and so do I,
as we each other fulfil.

But riches are the cause that now
you will take leave of me;
my friends shall go ahead while hers
left on the road shall be.

25 • And if I haven't a fortune so great
that soon would be forlorn,
I thank my God in Heaven that I
with honesty was born.

I do not rate her well enough
to think she can break the chain
that's bound us in all honesty,
little from that she'll gain.

Remember, my dear, beloved friend,
the wagging tongues which infer
that often we met secretly
in places we never were.
– *My ever dearest, do never forget me.*

Quite often when you were away
I took the defence of yours,
as at the time when you were far
away on the wilden moors.

Until the very end of time
my heart will remain to be true;
there isn't a single soul in the world
can turn me away from you.

30 • Longing is a great sorrow,
and me it's going to kill;
there never was any in all the world,
none that I trusted so well.

For when my eyes did see you,
I'd always joy in my heart,
and it did never enter my mind
that riches could keep us apart.

If I were wooed by the son of a king,
I would have thwarted his claim;
and so I think that another one
should do the very same.

If I were wooed by knights and squires,
with castles, gifts and ado,
I would not find a single one
I'd rather have than you.

How often at my own table,
at dinner, night, in the morn,
have I from friends and kinfolks
suffered from words of scorn?
– *My ever dearest, do never forget me.*

35 • Because of you, my dearest love,
because I to you belonged
and never thought of another
the friends of mine I wronged.

I know full well your heart is good,
and it is good to me,
and I shall in all my living days
love you in honesty.

Whatever the reason I love you so
with all my mind and might,
no other lives in all the world
on whom I'll set my sight.

Almighty God, you alone decide
what shall occur, so be it!
I'll never believe that it is true,
before I happen to see it.

I know full well that you are mine,
are mine as life is long,
and never shall you see the day
I'll trust a wagging tongue.

40 • And do you know, my dearest friend,
my anger is far stronger
than anything else – may our Lord
shame every scandal monger.

Our lot we place in the hand of God,
we place it in His care;
but my beloved, forget me not
wherever you may fare.
– *My ever dearest, do never forget me.*

And as we're always dear to each other
and equals, you and I,
then I shall never desert you till
my soul from my body shall fly.

Good night, good night, me dearest friend,
then travel far and wide,
I hope to God in His Paradise
you soon will be at my side.

Good night, good night, beloved mine,
I pray that you take care
that nobody with lies and tricks
shall catch you in their snare.

45 · May God in Heaven, the Almighty,
now steer your course and arm you,
whether you fare on land or sea,
that nobody shall harm you.

This poem isn't written
by me on banter bent;
so help me God in Paradise,
in earnest it is meant.

And I have written this poem down
out of a heart so true;
I pray you prove the same to me
without any hurt or rue.

I shall not sign my name to this,
you know it without being told;
our names have been written side by side
in honor manifold.
– *My ever dearest, do never forget me.*

Yes, they have been cut together
in metal so red and golden;
all the days I shall live on Earth
to you I shall be beholden.

50 • My poem has now come to an end,
I am with my writing through;
may God turn loss to victory,
and make it all come true.

51 • I wish the Lord may protect you,
also as many good-night,
as flowers grow on earth, and stars
in the heavens shed their light.
– *My ever dearest, do never forget me.*

69 THE NIGHTINGALE SENT TO THE KING
Langebek's Quarto Manuscript, 1571–80

You noble nightingale, godspeed!
with your winsome and crimson song,
fly to my master's royal seat
and tell him what does me wrong.
I suffer of love that burns and burns,
my pain is bitterly grim,
my heavy heart it twists and turns,
please, ask for mercy from him.

O noble crown, keep me in sight,
and turn your favor to me;
against your will and your regal might
but small my talent be.
Your rank is high, I'm forced to say,
while mine, I'm lowly born;
they are unlike as day and night,
if me you intend to scorn.

Oh, look at me with graciousness,
console me with your voice,
deliver me of love's distress,
be with me and let me rejoice.
For you I gladly suffer,
even if die I might;
therefore to you I offer
a prayer for help in my plight.

If you knew my heavy pain
and could my anguish see,
if I ventured to complain,
you might have mercy with me.
Don't let me suffer at length
for being poor and low,
but comfort me with your strength
and free me of ache and woe.

5 · My eyes they fairly shone
because of your regal look,
when you in the joust rode on,
a glove as keepsake I took.
Your weapons and coat of mail,
your shield and your noble lance
did on my heart prevail
with passion's dolor and pangs.

To you my heart is bound
by love that is fathomless,
I'm crushed into the ground
by passion's bitterness.
So manifold is my grief,
I know not what to do,
if you won't grant me relief,
that power belongs to you.

I never dared to show
my grief to any man;
if anyone should know
the reckless risk I ran
by loving such gentle blood,
I might be quite forlorn,
as it might be my lot
to suffer jeers and scorn.

So do not turn away,
this is my humble plea,
but pity me, I pray,
in all my misery.
If it would just come true
that I might see your face
and sometime be with you,
please, answer me with grace.

Beloved o'er any and all,
your smile is the joy of my eye;
if only I heard you call,
then I would gladly die.
May God come to my aid,
your peer I shall never be;
time's stopped for me, poor maid,
so full of misery.

10 · O nightingale, be faster
and hurry on your flight,
that you can tell my master
about my plight tonight;
that I am sorrowful for love
and pining misery,
for him alone I am thinking of,
beg him to be good to me.

70 DISAPPOINTMENT OVERCOME
Svaning's Manuscript I, about 1580

A fellow with looks that weren't too bad,
quite reasonable was he,
unbosomed himself and spoke to me
about his misery;
he told me that nobody else but I
next to God could bring him cheer;
that kind of words and many more
was all that I did hear.

His words they sounded very nice,
they went right to my heart;
I loved him well for a little while,
that I took pains to impart.
No force in the world could persuade me then
to think he wouldn't be loath
of playing me false if he had a chance,
despite his promise and oath.

He kept me going with merry tricks,
and thus I couldn't doubt
that we two sat on the top of the world,
and no one could shove me out.

I cheered him up with honeyed words
quite freely in his plight,
and so I gave him tit for tat,
that serves such rascals right.

He promised eternal fidelity,
but trickery he had planned;
and deep in my heart I didn't mind,
this I let him understand.
You reap what you sow at any time,
I know these words and tune:
a longing for him is gnawing my heart,
maybe I'll forget it soon.

5 • Although he surely has done me wrong,
I do not want to complain.
The war isn't won, for he will trick
still others again and again.
My heart has chosen another one,
let's see how my luck will appear;
I wish him the very best of luck,
the one who shall bring me cheer.

71 'TWAS ON A SATURDAY EVENING
Recording from the region of Aarhus, 1837

'Twas on a Saturday evening
I sat awaiting thee;
thou promised thou wouldst come, dear,
but didn't come to me.

And on my bed I lay, dear,
and cried so bitterly,
and every time I heard the door
I thought that it was thee.

I rose on Sunday morning
and cried so bitterly;
I thought that I would go to church
for there my love to see.

But when the church I entered,
my love I did not see;
for thou hadst gone another way,
thou wert deceiving me.

5 · Where canst thou gather roses,
where roses were not grown?
And love, where canst thou find it bloom,
where love was never sown?

72 THE JILTED MAID
Recording from Northern Zealand by A. P. Berggreen

A thousand thoughts I harbor,
I love the one that won't be mine;
while he is in joy's arbor,
all by myself I pine,
because I didn't get the one
I love and glorify;
and many scheming people
they are the reason why.

If I had never noticed
your face and your two eyes so blue,
if I had never gone to
the place that harbors you,
right happy would I then have been
and free from woe and pain;
but it will never happen
I shall be glad again.

Look at the pretty blossoms,
how they are lovely in the lea;
my heart dies in my bosom,
'cause he is not for me.
Yes, if I now should pine to death,
the grief your heart would find;
forever and forever
I have you on my mind.

4 · Far sooner would I wander
on dreary road in greatest plight
than I would live with people
who take in wiles delight.
The desert I will travel to
and there my tent put up,
for all my words are echoed
from every green treetop.

73 THE ROSE OF LOVE
Recording by C. Schütz, 1843

A lovely and wonderful summertime
with glory beneath and above,
it gladdens and heartens so many a one
with our Maker's love.
It brings the flower bevy on,
the rose's bed, so sweet and red,
envisage you anon.

'Mongst all the flowers one I know,
a rose, the perfect gem;
the lovely rose of mine does grow
on a delightful stem.
Though beautiful so many be,
I will declare in verity,
he outshines all the others.

His heart it is a Christian heart
without the least deceit;
his mouth does only truth impart,
his eyes are soft and sweet;
his cheek is like the rose so red,
his mouth with honey overlaid,
yes, he is fine and handsome.

Would only fortune grant that I
could keep this rose as mine;
my heart it blazes to the sky,
for him I yearn and pine.
When he's in sight, my heart is bright
and laughs with love and with delight
and doesn't let me rest.

[Here the writer inserts a similar quotation from Catullus and continues:]

I am making quite a bit of this song, because I deem it to be old or at least as *good* as old. Thus my punctiliousness. Besides, the lines "and on account of love's delight / it doesn't make me rest" may be the original wording, the more so as the girl neither understood the text, nor was she certain that it was the real one. pedantus, pedanta, pedantum.

(The informant who sang it for the writer, used the words: "it doesn't let me know" – know with the meaning "understand" – instead of "it doesn't let me rest").

5 • Wherever I may roam at day,
whatever I may do,
my thoughts they always turn your way,
and in the night-time, too.
And in my sleep so sweet and free
I dream about you happily
as if you were beside me.

6 · If all your beauty withered away
like flowers in a glen,
your pious soul would surely stay,
my ever dearest friend.
So comfort your anxiety:
as God ordains, so shall it be,
nobody can ever change it.

IV · ADDENDUM

13 · ADDENDUM

74 MEDIEVAL FRAGMENTS
Clerks' pen tests in diverse manuscripts

a: The Cologne Verse c. 1250 (Translation printed in the Notes)
iac wet en frugha i wærældet wære
hænna lif tha wil iac æræ

b: The Skåning Verse c. 1300
haui that skanunga ærliki mææn
toco vithær oræt aldrigh æn

c: The Rune Verse c. 1300
drømde mik en drøm i nat
um silki ok ærlik pæl

d: The Greenland Verse c. 1424, compare No. 21
Ther boer eeynh manh ij eyn Gronelands aa,
ooc Spieldehbedh mundhe hanyd heyde;
meer hawer han aff nidefildh
een hanh ha[w]er flesk hi[n]th feyde.
Nordhum driuer sandhen naa new new.

e: The Marsk Stig Chorus c. 1460, compare No. 14
fforthy stand landh j waadh

f: Lyric Prelude, 16. century
jak war for snimam wdhi en dans
iak sa twa roser standhæ

g: Parody-Rhyme, 15. century
megh haffuær drømet iæn drøm i nat
thet var om ien kat
thet och om ien hundh
och om ien trø[l?]

h: Humoristic Lines, c. 1500
Myn kære moder gører megh eyn grød
jak haffuer myn mødwm wti mith skød
thet kaller aa. . .

i: Aase and Karonelle, c. 1500
frw Osse oc frw K*a*ronelle(?)
the øuede thom   da*n*tzen

k: The Knight in Deerskin, c. 1450

Drømth haffuer mik om jomfrwer i alle naath.

Th*eth* wor herræ Peder,
ha*n* tal*e*r till swene tw:
"Kwnde i mik stolz Ose-lille
m*eth* fag*e*r talen fa?"
Drømt haffu*er* mik om jomfrwen alle nath.

Borth tha gynge the panszer-swene
alz th*e*r, stolz Ose-lille wor:
"My*n* herræ ha*n* holl*e*r weth sneke-bordh,
ha*n* will alth haffue idh*e*rt taall."
Drømth.

Swar*e*dhe ok stolz Ose-lille,
hwn swar*e*dhe th*e*r-till eth ordh:
"Th*eth* ær ængen jomfrw-seth,
ath gange till snecke-bordh. etc.

Th*eth* ær ængen jomfrw-seth,
ath ga*n*ge till snecke-bordh:
hen*ne* folgh*er* hiem bode lasth oc ska*m*,
swaa ma*n*thet hodigsos-ord."

5 · Ath*er* ko*m*me the pantzser-swene,
the sagde th*er* herræ i-fraa:
"Icke kwnde wij stoldz Ose-lille
m*eth* fag*er* talen faa."

"Kwnde i icke stoldz Ose-lille
m*eth* fag*er* ordh*en* faa:
tha skal jek far*e* i my*n* hiorte-ha*m*,
swaa wel skal jek he*n*ne faa."

7 · Th*eth* een ham wor aff hw[i]dit sølff,
th*eth* a*n*nith aff rødhe gwldh:
th*eth* wor h*er*re Pedh*er*,
ha*n* speller swaa frydhe-fuldh.

75 LAVE STISEN AND LADY ELINE
Langebek's Folio Manuscript, about 1630, compare No. 27

There was pretty Ellensburg,
just a child was the maid
when her father and mother
both of them passed away.
– *O great Lord, how you can change our sorrows.*

Father and mother they passed away,
brothers and sisters all;
but a knight so rich betrothed her
who Lavé Stisen was called.

He betrothed pretty Ellensburg,
she was a beautiful ward
whom he gave into his mother's care,
and then he went abroad.
– *O great Lord, how you can change our sorrows.*

There was Lavé Stisen,
going abroad was he;
there was Esben Ottosen
at home destined to be.

5 · There was Lavé Stisen,
his ship took off from land;
there was Esben Ottosen,
he rode his steed on the sand.

There was Esben Ottosen
swathed his head in skin;
when he came to the castle,
to Ellensburg he went in.

"Harken, Lady Ellensburg,
with favor you me behold;
a pretty shirt you sew for me,
embroidered nicely with gold."

"If I sewed you a pretty shirt,
embroidered nicely with gold,
that my betrothed would never like,
if he should be told."

Either of them knew not
that the serving maid
she stood hidden behind the door
and listened to what was said.

10 · It was the little serving maid
she wrote a letter by hand
and sent it to Lavé Stisen,
far off in foreign land.
– *O great Lord, how you can change our sorrows.*

Uttered Lavé Stisen
when he saw the chit:
"Help us, o Lord in Paradise,
what shall us now befit?"

There was Lavé Stisen,
home again he came;
his mother and his bespoken maid
came out to welcome him.

Together they walked inside,
as if they had fear for naught;
little knew fair Ellensburg
what Lavé Stisen thought.

"Welcome home, Lavé Stisen,
welcome, my husband to be!
Why did you stay in foreign countries
so long away from me?"

15 · "When long ago I went abroad,
so pure a maiden were you;
but now I have the tidings heard,
Esben Ottosen hankers for you."

"So help me God who dwells above
and also Christi mother:
I never had more to do with him
than if he'd been my brother."

He placed her in an empty room,
for three years 'twas her state;
he took the little serving maid
for his unwed mate.
– *O great Lord, how you can change our sorrows.*

To Ellensburg none was allowed
either to talk or go,
but for Sir Lavé's mother
who went to and fro.

Entered Sir Lavé's mother,
she was a lady upright:
"God's mercy with you, Ellensburg,
how your cheeks are white."

20 · Answered her fair Ellensburg,
she was so fine a maid:
"God help me, who is all alone,
now my father and mother are dead."

There was Sir Lavé's mother,
she dons her velvet and furs,
then she goes to the castle hall,
to that son of hers.

"Here you are, Lavé Stisen,
beloved son of mine,
will you wed your bespoken maid,
she is a maiden so fine?"

Answered her Sir Lavé,
an angry man was he:
"No, indeed, my mother dear,
that shall never be.

Harken to me, mother dear,
that shall never be.
This Sunday shall my wedding
to my mistress see."
– *O great Lord, how you can change our sorrows.*

25 · "If you hold your wedding now
to your unwed wife,
I wish to God in Paradise
you'll have a woeful life."

There was Lavé Stisen
he dons his velvet and fur,
then he goes into the room
to Lady Ellensburg.

"Harken, pretty Ellensburg,
you are so fair a maid:
you shall go to my chamber
and make my wedding bed."

On top she spread the silken sheet,
below the weave she spread:
"It is my mistress who shall sleep
happily in this bed.

I shall give her a pretty gown,
made of velvet blue;
one that's coarse and homespun
I shall give to you.

30 · I shall give my mistress
a golden belt to put on;
all that I am giving you
is a hempen one."

Answered Lady Ellensburg
with honor and purity:
"Whatever clothes you'll give me
shall be worn by me."
– O great Lord, how you can change our sorrows.

It was Sunday morning,
it was the holy day,
and Lavé and his mistress
wanted to be on their way.

His mistress stood in the chamber,
dressed in velvet blue;
fair Ellensburg stood outside
in homespun of greyish hue.

His mistress stood in the chamber
and put the gold belt on;
fair Ellensburg took the other,
that was the hempen one.

35 • Said Sir Lavé's mother,
she was in great distress:
"God's mercy with you, dear daughter,
in such a wedding dress."

So happy was the mistress
that she to the church should drive;
so woefully cried Ellensburg
that she was left outside.

They chanted the mass to the finish,
the text the priest did read;
Lavé Stisen followed
his mistress on his steed.

Entered the little page-boy,
dressed in his cloak so white:
"Now comes Sir Lavé's mistress
around the mountain side.
– *O great Lord, how you can change our sorrows.*

Her carriage she is laid with gold,
her horses are dapple-grey;
the like, fair Lady Ellensburg,
will never come your way."

40 · Then they took the mistress,
put her in the bridal seat;
it was Esben Ottosen
who brought her drink and eat.

They ate and drank for a little while,
but least the newly wed;
there was Lavé Stisen
he wanted to go to bed.

And they put the mistress
into her silken bed;
there was Lavé Stisen
eagerly pressed ahead.

There was Lavé Stisen's cloak
on the ground it fell;
Ellensburg she picked it up,
for she loved him well.

There was Lady Ellensburg
at once picked up the cloak;
then it happened that her belt
suddenly it broke.

45 · Said fair Lady Ellensburg,
she was so good a maid:
"That which should have stayed, it broke,
what ought to break, it stayed."
– O great Lord, how you can change our sorrows.

There was Lavé Stisen
with urgency he spoke:
"What was that which ought to last,
and what was it that broke?"

"'Twas my belt, Sir Lavé,
around my waist it broke;
but my heart that ought to break,
it carries still the yoke."

Answered her his mistress,
laughing with all her heart:
"Little harm would it have done,
if your heart fell apart."

Said Sir Lavé Stisen,
he was a man so staid:
"Harken, pretty Ellensburg,
I'm sorry for what you said.

50 · Harken well, my mistress,
and go away from me;
come to me, my bespoken wife,
you shall my sweetheart be."

And his mistress ran away,
an angry maid was she.
"Go to the priests and bring them here,
also the bishops three.

Go to the priests and bring them,
also the bishops two;
they shall marry me right away
to my maid so true."
– *O great Lord, how you can change our sorrows.*

And the priests and the bishops
to Lavé's house were led;
married they Lavé and Ellensburg
beside the wedding bed.

Ellensburg has triumphed
over distress and harm;
now she sleeps so happily
in Sir Lavé's arm.

55 · It was early morning,
at the first light of dawn,
when Sir Lavé's mother
to the bride house went on.

"Good morning, Sir Lavé Stisen,
good morning, my dear son,
with the little bride of yours
how did you get on?"

"I got on so happily
with my little bride,
and I rue that for my sake
she has suffered and cried."

"Harken, Lavé Stisen,
the best that can be done:
give your mistress for his wife
to Esben Ottosen."

59 · There is joy and gladness
where Sir Lavé abides;
he gave Esben his mistress
and two farms besides.
– *Oh great Lord, how you can change our sorrow.*

76 THE DICE GAME

Fragment from Western Jutland, by E. Tang Kristensen 1895; cp. No. 33

Did also know the ditty about the sailor who threw dice with a maiden in order to win her. He was a son of an English king.

I will ha' the maiden
whom I [won] at golden dice.

She wanted to give him one of her father's farms, but he would not listen to that. He had quite a nice name. Muddle-Kirsten from south of Aastrup knows the song. She lives way out at Great-Bog and knows many old ditties and sings nicely.

77 THE WEDDING OF THE FLY

Hans Mikkelsen Ravn's Rhythmologia, 1649; cp. No. 38

Lastly, some rhymes are provided with coda, others not. Without coda, outgrowth, appendage, or what else they can be called, are those rhymes that lack intermittent refrain or chorus. Among them are many spiritual and many secular, partly from life during war, in the country or in the towns, partly also love and humoristic songs and so on. Those songs have coda that are supplied with intermittent refrain or chorus. Intermittent refrains belong, according to the directives of the famous Scaliger (Poetry, Book II (also called Hylé) p. 186), to the art that is called intermittent.

That is the definition of those which can be removed, without the meaning being disturbed . . . [This kind of verse has either identical or changing choruses . . .] varied to the degree that the different verses obtain quite different endings. To them belongs the Fly-song where each stanza has two totally different choruses.

The gnat's forerunner rode up to the farm
– *the cranes they strum on their fiddles* –
there stood the fly in furs so warm
– *with flowers and with nettles.*

or:

The gnat's forerunner rode up to the farm
– *pyrum* –
there stood the fly in furs so warm
– *pyrum patrum nostrum.*

. . . Choruses like these have often a certain importance, they must not be empty, superfluous or alien to the theme, but may add grace, force, beauty or wit to the composition. Often they contain the whole thing, the main thought or some circumstance that elucidates the content. In that case, the chorus springs from the idea of the song, from its outcome or from the mood which the poet wants to emphasize; or from a special stanza, from which it then must develop as naturally as the brook streams from the spring.

78 FAITHLESSNESS
Anna Urop's Manuscript, about 1610

All honesty has faded
on Earth, and so has troth;
love has been dissipated
merely to sham and froth.
Flimflam and masquerading
from dawn to dusk you see
together promenading
with rotten piety.

Nobody can you swear by,
and words have little worth,
not far away nor nearby,
nor any place on Earth;
many a man without trouble
feign that they mean you well,
when it is all a bauble,
no meat, but only shell.

Before so many I trusted
and thought them friends to be;
it made me so disgusted,
brought evil and misery.
But it has oft been stated,
and it's so true, so true:
deception has prostrated
and smitten its master with woe.

4 • I am supposed to have lingered
in places where never I went;
my good name has been fingered,
to harm me they fully intend.
But I'll let every being
behave the way they please,
and I would like to see them
also let me in peace.

79 O LORD, O LORD, A HEART SO TRUE (Hymn)
H. C. Sthen's Wanderers' Book, about 1600, cp. No. 64

O Lord, O Lord, *a heart so true*
for you shall always be fain;
you saved me, and I belong to you,
and thus great praise you gain.
'Tis easy to tell,
you *love* us *well,*
you took our sins upon your*self*
when on the cross you were slain.

The love *that you have given me*
a chain between us has spun.
Now comes the devil *with perfidy*
and says *that he has won.*
You aren't, nay,
the *deceitful way,*
you will not leave me in dismay,
but let me hold your hand.

You fill me, Master, *with* misery,
if you want us to separate;
but *I* trust in *you* eternally,
the pain of my heart shall abate.
My heart's great woe
and life's hardship, too,
make day and night so slow, so slow,
my joy they'll devastate.

You promised by mouth and heart *before,*
and surely it stands, o Lord,
that you will love *me for evermore,*
you'll never break your word.
But if you chose
to reason close,
you'd know, no matter how it goes,
I never shall desert.

5 · Nobody in the world knows how
to stop my trepidation,
but God, if He desires now
to bring me consolation.
O Jesus sweet,
help in my need,
you died for our sins, indeed,
then let me gain salvation.

Amen.

V · NOTES AND INDICES

14 · NOTES

The following commentaries are divided into parts by asterisks: reference to sources, comments, and explanations of words (if any). The titles of five works are abbreviated throughout, see the list on page 295 for detailed explanation. However, the original source of the chosen version is given under the titles throughout the book. We only refer to the volume of *Danmarks gamle Folkeviser* when the version is found in an appendix and not in the main sequence of numbers.

I · BALLADS

1 · Folklore

1 · THE POWER OF MUSIC, page 31. Danish title and first line: *Tonernes magt* or *Harpens kraft (Hr. Peder han rider i gårde).* DgF 40 G (vol. X). ⁎ The ballad about the ogre in the river, whose evil designs defy all careful measures, but whose power, nevertheless, must give way to that of music, is apparently cast in one piece. However, historically, it is perhaps welded together from two parts: a tragic ballad of the older type, where the force of nature is impersonal and overpowering – as in the German tradition; and a ballad with roots in the myth of Orpheus, the Shetland King Orfeo (see Child 19; the harp of the older version has been supplanted by a wind instrument). Altogether the version is well built in its main features. Traditionally this ballad has several different choruses, the one quoted here is as authentic as the famous: "The strings are of gold. So deliciously he played for his maiden."

2 · THE ELF-SHOT, page 33. *Elveskud (Mangen rider rank og rød).* DgF 47B. ⁎ The ballad is known in many countries, with Brittany as the original center. It must be classified as belonging to the oldest stratum of ballads of sorcery. The tension between the mood of the ballad and that of the chorus is one of its main characteristics. Until the 1840's only Syv's version was known. For this reason the fame

and literary consequences of this ballad is connected with this. Syv's notes show him both as a linguist, a folklorist, and a clergyman. A passage omitted here shows that he was also a poet as he quotes a sonnet written by himself, on the occasion of a visit by King Christian IV (reigning 1588–1648) to the peninsula of Stevns in Sjælland.

3 · THE ELF HILL, page 35. *Elvehøj (Min fader han gav mig sadel og hest).* DgF 46Ca (vol. IV) according to Niels Jensen Vestergaard. Evald Tang Kristensen recorded quite a few versions at an early date; we quote one of them directly from his diary, but include verses 7 lines 2, 9, 10, and 12 from the combined version 46C – a procedure that seems permissible in this case. * The first-person-singular form and the admonition at the end point to the late Middle Ages as its time of origin; this is also suggested by the happy ending. Our version is similar to the one in Vedel's edition, 1591, but partially independent of it (v. 1). The chorus "Never since first I saw them" implies the continuation "have I been able to forget her". Digressing a little we allow ourselves to note the following: J. L. Heiberg's play, *The Elf-Hill, Elverhøi,* 1828, uses part of the legend about Christian IV and the hill on Stevns that is mentioned by Syv in his notes to No. 2. One of the characters sings No. 3 in a slightly revised version to a folk tune published in 1814. This play by Heiberg became a national patriotic play and in 1966 it had its 900th performance at The Royal Theater. The incidental music by Fr. Kuhlau uses genuine folk tunes, more or less reworked. Niels W. Gade's choral work, *The Elf-Shot, Elverskud,* 1853, another masterpiece of the romantic age, is not based on folk tunes, but its lyrics, written by C. K. F. Molbech, mirror the dark theme of No. 2 and uses quotations from other ballads, especially No. 3. * 4 *runes and books* corresponds to the old source's *books and runes,* which in this particular version, however, was transformed by the concept of the common people into *bage og ro:* bake and row.

4 · THE KNIGHT'S RUNES, page 37. *Ridderens runeslag (Hr. Peder og hr. Oluf de sidder over bord).* DgF 73A. * A sorcery ballad of later date. The characters are individualized, and the sorcery and its effects are partly symbolic. This version is selected for its lyrical excellence. Some of the modern versions are better in certain respects, there being no confusion as to runes, harp or horn, nor contradiction between stanzas 5 and 32, and a fixed ending without verses of newer date such as 38–39.

5 • THE FEATHERED MAIDEN, page 41. *Jomfru i fugleham (Jeg ved vel, hvor en skov hun stander).* DgF 56C. ∗ The first three stanzas are nothing less than the greatest description of nature in Danish ballad literature. They may, however, have been transferred from other sources (see No. 63). The story of the metamorphosis varies very much in the different versions; some of the details are obscure (10?). ∗ 4,2 is taken from source D.

6 • THE BURIED MOTHER, page 43. *Moderen under mulde (Lidel Ellen hun hviler i Himmerige).* DgF 90Øa (vol. X), according to Sidsel Jensdatter of Gjellerup parish, one of Evald Tang Kristensen's most talented informants. ∗ One of the famous dramas of Danish romanticism, *Svend Dyrings Huus,* by Henrik Hertz (1837), is based on this ghost ballad, which was highly popular in later tradition. Our version combines independence and loyalty to the oldest group of versions. ∗ 4 and 9 express common superstition of the time. 25 and 26 ought to have been followed by a third morning stanza about the rooster so white.

7 • THE TALKING HARP, page 46. *Den talende strengeleg (I Odense by der boede en mand).* DgF 95F, according to "Myse-Ellen" of Tjæreby parish. ∗ The Danish versions of the ballad are all of a late date and none too good; but the motif – the instrument that reveals of whose body it is made – is a very old international folk story motif ("the two sisters"). ∗ 9–12 follow 13–16 in the original, but are placed here as in DgF. 10 *life* is a correction of the original *land* (otherwise the small corrections by Grundtvig are not followed). 18,1 added by Grundtvig. 18,2 has possibly not been sung, but just spoken.

2 • *Christianity*

8 • ST. OLAV'S RACE, page 49. *Hellig Olavs væddefart (Kong Oluf og hans broder).* DgF 50B. ∗ "This song about St. Olav, King of Norway, is a poetical and not a historical poem," Vedel correctly remarks. There is a rich growth of legends about St. Olav, the Norwegian king killed in 1030 (owner of the vessel "Ox"), who was thought to resemble the thunder-god Thor and often confused with Olav Trygveson, the equally famous king of Norway who introduced Christianity there (owner of the ship "Long Serpent", here: "Snake"). In the unhistoric

episode in this ballad the piety and strength of the saint are merely a veneer covering pre-Christian features. Illustrations to the song are found in Danish church frescos; thus it is not necessarily of Norwegian folk tradition through the centuries. The verse form is a concatenated stanza that perhaps reflects a singing technique with two leaders. It has been discussed thoroughly in our time. ⁎ 22 *Skaneyarfjöll* is a mountain range near Trondheim, and this is the probable meaning of the name *Skaanerknolde* in the version used. 25, 3–4 may be incomprehensible to the reader, as, perhaps, it also was to the recorder. According to version A it should have been: "the arrow fell behind the mast" – thus the speed of the boat was so great that an arrow, shot in the same direction as the course of the vessel, landed behind the point from which it had been released(!).

9 • THE INFANT JESUS, STEPHEN AND HEROD, page 52. *Jesusbarnet, Stefan og Herodes (En jomfru ren oprunden er).* DgF 96 with the accompanying prose in Jørgen Olrik's translation, see Erik Pontoppidan: *Everriculum ... i. e.* "A broom for sweeping out the old leaven, or the still existing and hereby exposed remnants of both paganism and Papism in the Danish lands" (1736), as reprinted in *Danmarks Folkeminder* 27 (1923). The nota benes were inserted at the superstitious passages by Pontoppidan (see Child 22, St. Stephen and Herod). ⁎ The only Danish version of a legend song with parallels in English and especially in Swedish (Staffansvisor). It contains both adoration of the Virgin Mary and sundry legendary characteristics. The special connection between the saint of Boxing-day and the horses (v. 6) is no longer regarded as deriving from pre-Christian ideas; on the other hand the cock as herald of the birth of Christ, *i. e.* light's victory over darkness, has roots in its ancient role as an oracle bird and an expeller of evil (the weathercock). – The song ought to have been placed in chapter 8, as – unlike the omitted DgF 97 – it is not in the form of a ballad.

10 • THE SOUL OF THE CHILD, page 54. *Barnesjælen (Og hvordan mon græsset på jorden skulde gro).* DgF 107A. ⁎ In Denmark found only in comparatively late versions. Its Catholic character is preserved even more conspicuously in a Norwegian version: here it is the Holy Virgin who speaks to the child; in a Spanish legend the child saves his father who is a highwayman.

3 · *Kings and Nobles*

11 · VALDEMAR AND TOVELIL, page 57. *Valdemar og Tove (Tovelil står i hendes faders gård).* DgF 121A. * Grundtvig proved in his introduction to this ballad that the Tove legends must be attached to the Danish King Valdemar I the Great (d. 1182), and not to King Valdemar IV Atterdag ("Another Day") who died in 1375. Our version shows unreliability by letting Canute (Knud VI) be a bastard like Christoffer, while he was in reality the son of Valdemar I and Queen Sophia. In any case, the ground is anything but solid as the ballad is devoid of historically established occurrences and characters and must be regarded as springing from Franco–English sources dealing with Henry II of England (d. 1189) and arbitrarily connected with the royal house of Denmark. The motif itself, husband–wife–mistress, is common in our ballads. The Tove ballad is widely distributed in Scandinavia; its composition and details vary so much that it must have been consciously reshaped. The statement of the chorus, that the king loves both women *med raade, i. e.* consciously, points to the oldest tradition. The ballad kept rather neutral in regard to jealousy, and the possibility of a balanced relationship between the two women was not an idea alien to the epoch. * 26 must be the queen's words. 36,2 is missing in the original and constructed by Grundtvig after 37,2. 39 must be the king's words.

12 · QUEEN DAGMAR'S DEATH, page 60. *Dronning Dagmars død (Dronning Dagmar ligger udi Ribe syg).* DgF 135A. * History's judgment of the two queens of King Valdemar II Sejr (d. 1241; *Sejr:* Victory), the Bohemian Dragomir (d. 1212), and the Portuguese Berenguela (d. 1221), was formed so early that it must have been based on facts or, at any rate, on contemporary opinion. The unhappy conditions prevailing during the successive reigns of Bengerd's three sons, Erik Plovpenning (Plough-tax), Abel and Christoffer I (1241–59), may have darkened their mother's name after her death and emphasized the virtues of Dagmar. The ballad about Dagmar's death, colored by Catholicism to an unusual degree, presents a difficult point: Canute (Knud) was the natural son of Valdemar and the widow of the Sjælland chieftain Esbern Snare (d. 1204). Perhaps he was pretender to the crown 1245, and the ballad can thus be regarded as a current polemic poem of the time, especially if one substitutes *my* with *your* in v. 22–23. It is also a possibility that the name Canute appears instead of the name of Dagmar's son Valdemar (III, the Young: d. 1231). If so,

the tenor loses its political sharpness. This ballad is looked upon as one of the greatest and most beautiful; it is also regarded as being very old, perhaps one of the oldest in quatrains. There are various differences between the two old versions as regards details and place names. Vedel, who owned the Svaning manuscript, made several additions to the version used here. ⁎ 1 *Dagmar* means *dag-mø* (day-maiden), the name of honor constructed by popular etymology and given to Dragomir. 2 *Ribe* is corrected to *Rise* by Vedel. 4–5: in version B she is called Kirsten Eskildsdatter and is just a midwife; our source indicates semi-magic formularies; the Holy Virgin's Book is a collection of legends. 6,3 *verily, in all truth I say* is a stock phrase often used to fill in the third line of the quatrain. A variant by Vedel says: "She could not see the light of the chandelier, so full of tears were her eyes." 9 *Gullandsburg:* the island of Gotland, east of Sweden, belonged to Denmark 1361–1645, and was the eastern outpost of the realm; thus the name is added at a later date. 24 orig. *striger:* stripes? headdress? The Middle Ages took a more serious look at sumptuousness in dress and finery than later eras.

13–16 · THE MARSK STIG BALLADS, page 64–71. DgF 145A–O. ⁎ The Danish King Erik V Glipping was murdered on February 11, 1286. The Marsk (Lord High Constable) Stig Andersen was pointed out as leader of the plot. (He is called *Marsti* in the ballads, the conventional fusion of the title *Marsk* and the given name *Stig.*) He and eight others were outlawed in 1287, but he returned to Hjelm (pron.: yelm), a diminutive island off East Jutland, from where he made war on the government until his death in 1293. This was naturally one of the great events of the time; but the murder case has never been fully solved. Its monument is "The long Marsk Stig Ballad", DgF 145A, which, however, cannot be regarded as primary in relation to the smaller and quite different ballads, but merely as a literary fusion of these; recently, Helge Toldberg has tried to prove that it was compiled by A. S. Vedel. Here we print four of the smaller ballads, found only in the song books of the 16th–17th centuries, while another ballad, harmless and attached unhistorically to the daughters of Marsk Stig, continued to be highly popular (DgF 146, omitted here).

13 · MARSTI AND HIS WIFE, page 64. *Marsk Stig og hans hustru (Marsti han ud af landet for).* DgF 145C. ⁎ A doubtful tradition about King Erik Glipping's immoral behavior was made the basis of the seduction theme of this ballad and thus for the whole group, possibly formed on the basis of foreign prototypes. This is quite unhistorical –

a poetic personalization and motivation of the events. The fortification of Hjelm is placed earlier than the regicide, which is not mentioned at all, but is presupposed to have been executed by the Marsk. This is the latest ballad of the group, but is, nevertheless, supposed to have influenced the Niels Ebbesen ballad of ca. 1340. This ballad and the following have been provided with a string of corrections and additions by Vedel. * 4,3 ironical. 11 *Reval and Ri,* orig. *Reffuell och Rin* (i. e. Riga): Estonia was conquered and christianized by Denmark in 1219, but sold in 1340. Reval, but not Riga, belonged to Denmark at the time of the ballad, but Marsk Stig did not fight there. 13 is rather freely translated. 15 *guns:* not known in the 14th century.

14 • THE KING'S MURDER, page 66. *Kongemordet (Der er så mange i Dannemark).* DgF 145 G. * The only ballad of the group that supports king and country. There is not a hint as to the identity of the perpetrators of the murder, only general political unrest is given as the reason. The ballad is undoubtedly contemporary and thus adds a national quality to the esthetic. On the basis of an unknown source Vedel made several corrections in the manuscript that had been written for him; among others, two whole stanzas, quoted in brackets. * 5A *Ranild:* when King Erik had sought shelter for the night in the barn at Finderup in Jutland, and the disguised conspirators forced their way in to him, he was defended by his attendant Rane Jonsen. One source testifies to this; but the ballad author's insinuation that it was only a mock defense tallies with what came out in court, and Rane was banished together with the other eight. 10 *Erik* is inserted by Vedel instead of the meaningless *Canute;* it points to Erik Menved (1274–1319), the twelve year old royal prince who became king after the murder of his father.

15 • THE BANISHMENT, page 68. *Landsforvisningen (Marsti han vågner om midjenat).* DgF 145F. * This little ballad may have been written while the Marsk was still alive; its distinguishing feature is the last stanza about Hjelm; but it treats the actualities quite freely in its partisanship to him. There is not a word about the relationship between the Marsk's wife and the king, neither is Marsk Stig depicted as guilty. The introductory prophetic dream is a well-known motif in the poetry of the Middle Ages. In the A-text and in Vedel's edition the song is placed at the time before the Marsk's declaration of open hostilities. * 9 *Christoffer* was born in 1276, but did not become king until after his brother, Erik Menved. 13 The island Hjelm (helmet) has been furnished with castle towers, that look like horns on a helmet.

16 · THE OUTLAWS, page 70. *De fredløse (De vare vel syv og syvsindstyve).* DgF 145K. ⁎ This short episode, the only couplet in the group, is highly damaged, and possibly only a fragment. There is a slight variation in the chorus, but here, as is usual in all the manuscripts, it has only been written in greatly abbreviated form after each stanza. Again the hero is Marsk Stig, here the dauntless and resourceful central figure among the outcasts. ⁎ 1 The one hundred and forty seven *(syv og syvsindstyve)* has crept in from another ballad; Ernst von der Recke restores it cautiously and plausibly as: "Seven, each on his steed / they gathered on a heath: / 'Where shall we go? What path? / The king looks at us with wrath.'"

17 · NIELS EBBESEN, page 71. *(Greven drog i Danmark ind).* DgF 156F, *It Hundrede Vduaalde Danske Viser* (One hundred selected Danish songs), Ribe 1591, with Vedel's own introduction. ⁎ Costly and futile attempts to assert the king's authority in Denmark led after 1320 to the country's total bankruptcy; and in 1332–40 we have the sole interregnum in the history of Denmark; the whole country was divided between the two Holstein counts Johan II the Mild and Gerhard III the Bald-headed, and held in pawn by them. The latter's severe reign in Jutland was terminated when the local and little known squire and nobleman, Niels Ebbesen, with a band of men broke into his quarters in Randers on April 2, 1340, and killed him. Taking an unconventional and materialistic point of view, the Danish historian Erik Arup writes: "This assassination could no more than most of the other political murders in the history of the world change the natural outcome of historic events." This is not the common opinion. The revolt of the Jutland nobles against the occupation by the Holstein counts and the settlement made by the sons of the murdered count with Valdemar (IV Atterdag), the pretender to the Danish throne, are as a matter of fact regarded as the beginning of the latter's rule after the interregnum. The homage to him and his wedding took place in the spring of the same year. Niels Ebbesen was killed at Skanderborg on November 2 the same year, when the Jutland insurrection was quelled. – The ballad about Niels Ebbesen is probably a personification of a political conflict. This feature and others (such as the dialogue with his wife, copied after the Marsk Stig ballad) and the obscurity of certain statements, are poetic license, further differentiated and contradictory in the various versions. The poem, however, is not lacking in suggestions about Niels Ebbesen as a popular and national figure, a point of view that later on prevailed and which could not have been unknown to

the poet. "That the chorus, for once, is missing in all versions, indicates that the ballad has been on a higher level than usual: It is not a dance-ballad, but a piece of political and national poetry," says Ernst Frandsen. – There has been general agreement that this ballad is based on historical events, but some doubt arose from the extensive research to which it has been submitted since Grundtvig's pioneering publication of it in 1862. There is hardly any doubt about its contemporaneousness, and on account of its theme, characterizations and elementary tension, it will always hold an exceptional status among our historical ballads and in Danish poetry as a whole. – A popular-traditional point of view has also determined our choice of version. Anders Sørensen Vedel was not a philological publisher, but a competent ballad editor who liberally supplemented and smoothed out the sources. Nevertheless, this ballad about the best known event of the 14th century is given here in Vedel's version, the only form in which it was generally known until one hundred years ago; thus, we also quote Vedel's introduction. With the exception of this version the ballad is known only in manuscripts, mainly those used by Vedel; it is unknown in broadside or any other form. ⁎ Introduction, headline: *Jepson,* Vedel's text spells it Ebbissøn. *He challenged him honestly:* in reality it was the other way round and the count challenged Niels Ebbesen. 1 *banners* denotes the size of the army; there were possibly 11000 troops, with serious pillaging and still worse rumors following their advance. 4 *peaceful* (road) Vedel misunderstood the old *felighed* (safe conduct) as *fredlighed.* 11 It is clear to the count that Niels Ebbesen's quiet answer may be a subterfuge, but it looks as if the latter only little by little has become incited to break off the relationship. 26–28 are important stanzas: the count stands for a binding feudal system; Niels Ebbesen maintains the older point of view of the Danish nobles: that an allegiance could be withdrawn at will (compare 50 and 54), and that Anders Frost has been loyal to the count as long as it was his duty; he could not answer for Niels Bugge (24,1). 35, 1–2 refer to a humoristic proverb: he is much afraid who dares not tremble. 42 *wife:* more correct than Vedel's *mother;* the episode is free invention, as mentioned. 57 *brother* should have been *son.* 60 *Vejle* (originally *Vedel*) and *Kolding* are towns in Jutland far to the south of Randers. 65 *Klaus Krumdige:* the count's youngest son. 68,2 an unfortunate complementary line. 70 *yellow locks:* this shows the strong grip of the clichés of the ballad language on the story about the murder of the *bald-headed* count. 71,2 *with drums they called the men,* possibly also meaning: "with noble boldness ... to proclaim the murder" (Recke), or: the alarm of the Holsteins. 73 *Ove Hals,* or rather *Hase,* was the father-in-law of Niels Ebbesen's brother, for which reason Niels Ebbesen tries to avoid a fight with him. 76, 3–4 this curious statement, inserted clumsily after the so-called "day-version" of the ballad had been made, contradicts all other sources and is contrary to common sense; one chronicle states that Niels Ebbesen made the attack at night with 47 men, of whom one was killed, and mentions the famous episode of the ruined bridge. 82–83 typical final stanzas by Vedel, magnificent but foreign to the ballad style, although not totally alien to the sources; the original ending is uncertain. Stanza 81 is the most famous.

18 • THE EAGLE SONG, page 84. *Ørnevisen* or *Christian den anden og adelen (Alle små fugle, i skoven er).* DgF 173b. * Christian II (1481–1559, reigned 1513–23) is the most singular royal figure in the history of Denmark. The highly talented and enterprising man's progressive and ruthless policies brought him into conflicts with the nobles: when these revolted in Jutland, the king left Denmark. When he tried to retake Norway (which at that time was under Danish sovereignty) in 1531, King Frederik I guaranteed him a safe conduct for the negotiations, but broke the agreement and made him prisoner of state for the rest of his life. – This song is almost outside the boundaries of the ballad genre, to which its solid allegory is alien. Nevertheless, it is found in all traditional selections and cannot be left out of this broader anthology, as it demonstrates how an old form may be filled with new contents. The allegory, a well-known satiric weapon in other genres, is easily recognized: the small birds, etc. are the town people and peasants, the host of hawks the nobles, the eagle Christian II. The ballad is a piece of partisan literature from one end to the other, from the time of the king's exile in 1523 to his imprisonment in 1531. Modern research has shown that the "popular" poems of that time were often deliberate propaganda emanating from the chancellery of a king or from the personal coterie of a nobleman. However, it cannot be proved that this is the case here. * 2,1 inserted from the other version. 8 *host of hawks:* unclear word forms in the sources imply that this is a pun on the similarity in Danish between *høge-hær* (hawk host) and *høje herrer* (high gentry). 16 *I pity them* is absolutely foreign to the ballad style, in which even a narrating first-person is regarded as criterion of late origin, as in No. 3, The Elf-Hill. A narrator who reasons, is inconceivable.

19 • FREDERIK II IN THE DITMARSH, page 87. *Frederik den anden i Ditmarsken (Kong Fredrik han rider i Ditmarsken ind).* DgF 175K (vol. X). * While the majority of our most important historical ballads are not echoed in later popular song, this anecdote, well narrated, but totally unhistorical, has retained an extraordinary popularity right up to this century. The story seems to be that the conquest of the West-Jutland region Ditmarsken was prepared by the king's personal espionage (v. 2), interrupted by his opponents' recognition of his cutlery with the royal initials (v. 5). The chorus is a counterpart to DgF 169, that tells about King Hans and his unsuccessful attempt to conquer Ditmarsken in 1500, with the following chorus: "The Danish nobles, they lost their lives indeed." – This is the last of the regular historical ballads, possibly from about 1600.

4 • Saga and Myth

20 • SVEND NORMAND, page 89. *Svend Normand* or *Svend Vonved (Svend Normand sidder i bure).* DgF 18A; compare Child No. 1: Riddles wisely expounded. * In most versions the hero's name is *Vonved;* it is perhaps the same word as *vanvid* (madness) and is appropriate to the obscurity of this isolated ballad. Its Western Scandinavian and, possibly, Celtic sources are unknown and its basic idea, with the many violent episodes, is anything but clear. The ballad has acquired its popularity by the incorporation of a series of ancient, international riddle forms (see *Danske Studier* 1945). * 6 It is the mother who speaks, compare No. 31. 23 *moorland house,* free translation: original *hov,* English *hovel* (15th century, unknown origin). 28 *parties* original *sale,* halls. 29 *the drum,* original *thraann,* meaning doubtful, has been interpreted as *trane* (crane) at an early point of the transmission; it is possible that *drum,* too, is a misinterpretation, but it is supported by the Faroese versions,

21 • ANGELFYR AND HELMER KAMP, page 92. (*Ove han bor i Udes-kær).* DgF 19A. * The subject of this well-constructed ballad is also found in the Icelandic sagas and in a variant in Saxo's Latin chronicle of Denmark from about 1200. The Western Scandinavian names of the brothers are Angantýr and Hjálmarr Kappi (fighter), and the battle ground Samsø, an island east of Jutland. The peculiarity of the ballad, however, is that the three main characters are members of one family. This may be called a misunderstanding, but it is in the

spirit of ballads and is the very reason for the father's terrible act of revenge; v. 11, however, suggests that the rivals are not brothers. One of the stanzas has, under peculiar circumstances, been handed down from as far back as the Middle Ages, see No. 74d. * *Udes-ker* = *odders-kær* = otter's pond.

22 • HAVBOR AND SIGNE, page 96. *(Havbor konge og Sivord kong')* DgF 20B. * This famous ballad is a good example of the old subjects and much later origin of the heroic ballad. The ancient myths about the Siger-house in the mid-Sjælland royal town Ringsted indicate an earlier date than the Skjoldung house (Hroar, Helge, Hrolf) in Lejre at Roskilde; these events were already put into poetry in the ancient lay that Saxo transmitted in Latin about 1200. But the late-medieval ballad has only brought to light the love of two human beings from the welter of family and fate conflicts contained in the myth, and has provided the two old-fashioned clear-cut characters with noble sentiments, as in v. 41–42. Generally the heroic ballads are a West-Nordic ballad group; it is a much debated question whether this seemingly Danish jewel, with its widespread popularity all over Scandinavia, is an exception to the rule; recent research, however, supports the hypothesis of its West-Nordic origin. * 25,4 does not rhyme in this version; other sources have "with falcon on your hand" or similar clichés with a near-rhyme. 38,4 *while with the bedpost he won:* he won with the bedpost as a weapon. 43 *Paradise* is an anachronism, of the sort that now and then appears in early and later ballad tradition. 47 The revenge is alien to other versions. 51 and 53 are the king's words.

23 • SVEND FELDING, page 103. *(Det var hr. Svend Felding).* DgF 31A. * The growing German influence on ways and customs in the late Middle Ages has perhaps urged a Danish swain or squire to compose this ballad with its genuinely humorous nationalistic boasting; he knew the clichés pertaining to the joust from other ballads. Many shared the opinions of the poet: Svend Felding is a folklore figure, no end of myths and localities are attached to him. The story itself is neither original nor unique. No refrain. * 16 *pound:* a varied but usually large measure of corn. 21 *quarter:* six inches. 23,3 not until now does he understand that it is a plea to have the gird strapped less tightly. 27 *the holy wafer:* this Christian feature is indispensable in the story and aids in determining its time and composition. 32,4 *condoned:* in the hereafter.

•

5 • *Love and Death*

24 • NILUS AND HILLELIL, page 109. *(Det var bolder hr. Nilus).* DgF 325 (the A-text, based on Ab). ⁎ The force of the description of nature in v. 3–4 (which may be the ballad's original beginning) can best be appreciated if one remembers that even terse expressions of this sort are almost unprecedented in the ballad style: these expressions have faithfully followed the ballad in West Jutland, in Telemark (Norway), and in Småland (Sweden), while the ballad did not take root in other and more fertile regions. The characterization corresponds to this; it belongs to the early harsh ballad of chivalry at its height. The place names are too vague to be of help in the determination of time and area. ⁎ 5 *ride we* = if we rode, 6 = let us ride. 6,4 in contrast to Nilus she does not understand how firmly her uncle is committed to blood vengeance. 11,4 no further mention of details.

25 • EBBE SKAMMELSEN, page 113. *(Skammel han bor sig nør udi Thy).* DgF 354C. ⁎ The story of this ballad, generally recognized as the principal ballad of chivalry, is firmly fixed, but the details vary in an interesting manner, although too much stress ought not to be placed on the psychological interpretation of the differences. Axel Olrik's congenial notes and editing of the ballad (in DgF VI) have almost tied the hands of his successors, and few will deny that the old version A (36 stanzas) is the best of the genuine versions. We have, however, after much deliberation, selected another version in order to show that the poem also can be and most often is broader in its composition than it is usually seen, without it, for this reason, ceasing to be a masterpiece in its genre. – Ebbe's affinity to the Strange and Hvide families and his historicity have never been established. The ballad has obtained a legendary ending in a few versions, where Ebbe roams around in chains that are broken and fall off when he passes Peter's grave, as proof that he has been forgiven. But our last stanza is undoubtedly the true ending, from which the chorus develops in a natural way (see No. 77). This ballad is also found in Sweden, but although detailed localizations advise caution, it is definitely Jutlandish. Furthermore, version A, which used to be regarded as coming from Skåne (now a part of Sweden) is connected with Jutland (see DgF X with the results of Kr. Hald's studies which are of later date than this book in its original, Danish edition). ⁎ 1 *merry and well to do:* thus v. 2 of this version is unfortunate. 28 is here, as by Olrik, inserted from a variant. 30,3–4 is an infraction of the classical ballad's objec-

tivity. 36 in fact a gallery that led from the main hall to the bride's chamber; a nobleman near to the family held the torch for the bride; later the bridegroom was followed the same way. This ceremony was, also legally, the climax of the festivity, and the situation is thus logical.

26 • TORBEN'S DAUGHTER AND HIS SLAYER, page 120. *Torbens datter og hendes faderbane (Vi vare så mange søskende små).* DgF 288. * The smaller Stockholm manuscript (1641) named after the place where it is kept, contains the only existing version. Its quality is undeniable and its great age highly plausible. What takes place between the two main characters – love at first sight – is the essence of the ballad, but the conditions leading up to it are ambiguous. If, however, the initial extended chorus is regarded, not as an elegiac reference to Torben's daughter and her otherwise unmentioned brothers and sisters, but, as suggested by Ejnar Thomsen (see DgF X), as a reference to the children of Torben's victim, then the ballad tells about the attempt of their adult kinsmen to procure indemnity for them; their wrong estimation of the old-fashioned solid peasant's economic status – at a time, when a more knightly upper class was beginning to develop; and the slayer's alternative choice, to marry the daughter of the murdered man, whose kinsmen were now in duty bound to seek revenge by his breaking of the peace and his killing instead of agreeing to negotiate as offered. But other interpretations are also possible.

27 • LAVE STISEN AND LADY ELINE, page 122. *Lave Stisøn og fru Eline (Det var Lave Stisøn).* DgF 259A, recorded ca. 1600 by the Reverend Anders Sivenssön of Österslöv, in the district af Villand, Skåne, and sent to Ole Worm 1624. Reports of this kind from clergymen were important for Ole Worm's pioneering activities as an archeologist and antiquarian, but it is regrettable that they so seldom brought returns of this quality. * The highly solid and clear ballad is known only in Denmark and may well be a true story. It is included here on account of its quality, while we offer a longer version for methodic reasons, as No. 75. * 4,3–4 the ballad's prevalent expression for a woman's love for a man.

28 • CAROL ALGOTSON, page 124. *Karl Algotsøn (Hr. Karel red sig op på land).* DgF 182I (vol. X); as to the source see notes No. 47. * This ballad belongs to a group placed in DgF as a supplement to Danish historical songs, as they deal with persons from Swedish

history, but are not found in Swedish tradition. The ballad's historical connection with the deeds of the nobleman Carol Algotson, ca. 1290, has been neither proved nor disproved. When we place it among the ballads of nobility, it is not in order to be partisan on this point, but because its qualities in this connection have nothing to do with the characters, who are almost unknown in Denmark. The tension is created by the gamble lost to a perfectly cold and unyielding avenger, to a "serene and re-experienced anger that is impossible to hold back, because it lacks all ability for losing its temper" (Karl-Ivar Hildeman in DgF X). The place names vary in the records and are not to be relied on.

29 • THE WOMAN-MURDERER, page 127. *Kvindemorderen (Ulver han gilde stalt Vænelil).* DgF 183A. See Child 4 Lady Isabel and the Elf-Knight. ∗ This sinister ballad is of international renown, in highly different forms, of course, and has been the subject of several books and treatises. It seems to have originated in the Netherlands; one of the main "currents" goes to France and from there to the British Isles; another current goes via Germany to Scandinavia. It seems that Walloon emigrants took the French version to Hungary, where the story has adopted features from the ancient Hungarian (Ugrian) epic, *e. g.* the de-lousing request, v. 26, a sign of intimacy. The seducer has, in the Nordic ballads, all but lost his character as a supernatural being, and the song is therefore regarded as belonging to the ballads of chivalry, though not typical of them. Several other features are well preserved, despite the fact that the beginning is mixed with other ballads. ∗ 27 the improbability of his going to rest after having divulged his evil plans, is best explained by her making him sleep by runes or other magic; thus *it wasn't a pleasant nap.*

30 • BIRTH IN THE GROVE, page 130. *Fødsel i lunden* or *Redselille og Medelvold (Rosenelle hun danste på gulvet så brat).* DgF 271Q, see Child 15 Leesome Brand. ∗ More than one hundred versions of this ballad are found, most of them recorded after 1840. The great age of the story in Scandinavia is proved, however, by a couple of poor versions in the aristocratic song books which can be clearly shown to be side-branches of the original. The best choice of names is Redselille and Medelvold (Rosenelle and Medvel in this version) which, together with the German parallels to the ballad, attests to its origin. In the numerous sources the names undergo many changes.

31 • SVEND IN THE ROSE GARDEN, page 133. *Svend i Rosengård (Hvor har du været så længe)*. DgF 340A. See also DgF X, with references to important recent research. ✱ Although the story of this ballad precedes its beginning and possibly continues after its ending, and we thus have only a string of riddle questions and answers (in themselves far older than the poem as in No. 20) to stress the murderer's indelible sin, it belongs, nevertheless, together with its Nordic and English parallels (Child 13 Edward) to the most admired specimens of these countries' folk poetry. Its background is indefinable; it simply passes into the chivalry group, although it is tempting to classify it as a mythical ballad. In early versions one recognizes a knightly setting, in later ones a peasant environment. *Rose garden* seems to mean cemetery, which the singer possibly has not understood.

6 • *Humor and Sadness*

32 • THE MAIDEN'S MORNING DREAM, page 135. *Møens morgendrømme (Liden Vesterland blev født om en aftensmål)*. DgF 239V (vol. X). ✱ This pretty fairy-tale-like ballad has many versions; a chorus such as "But the Wenders laid siege to the castles" and the mentioning of the Wenders' king (in the Danish text treated as a name: *Hr. Vendelkong)* keep alive the memory about the Slavic nation, the Wenders, who lived where Eastern Germany is today, and raided the southern shores of Denmark during the early Middle Ages, until 1167. This fact has, however, not impressed itself on any realistic poetry. It is of further interest, that the ballad perhaps contains a hint of the legend that William of Malmesbury tells about King Athelstan's birth, see Aage Kabell, referred to in DgF X. The version is characteristic and important. The name *Vesterland* is only found here and in version A from a noblewoman's ballad book.

33 • THE DICE GAME, page 137. *Terningspillet (Der stander en skøn ridder i kongens gård)*. DgF 238U (vol. X). ✱ This highly popular ballad is nowadays only generally known in quatrain forms. However, a small couplet group exists, where the young man is neither a roaming journeyman nor a sailor, but a knight, who after bad luck in three games goes into the yard, where he hears a voice from heaven and then wins the fourth game. These versions (and especially the one selected here from one of the rare peasant song books that bear witness to the popular dissemination of the older knightly ballads) are

perhaps nearer to the original text of the ballad, which has been in much dispute in Scandinavia. The chorus does not belong to the ballad.

34 • THE DEAR ROBE, page 139. *Den dyre kåbe (Det var skønnen jomfru).* DgF 231A. * A merry little song, hardly of Danish origin.

35 • SISTER WOOS BROTHER, page 141. *Søster beder broder (Sammen sidder de søskend to).* DgF 437B. * This song stands quite isolated in the world of ballads, with its vibrant, picturesque eroticism and its extremely delicate subject; a comparatively late period is the background of its sensibility and language; there is nothing left of a plot. A good reader outside the circle of professionals, the artist Niels Skovgaard, wrote in plain words to his friend Axel Olrik after reading DgF VII: "I guess that the dialogue between sister and brother is the most poetic of them all." Version A ends with the brother's demand that she makes penitence for her sinful thoughts.

36 • THE YOUNG MAN'S DREAM, page 143. *Ungersvends drøm (Jeg drømte om natten, som jeg lå).* DgF 509A. * Here the ballad form is still more hollowed out than in No. 35. This song, perhaps, belongs to Chapter 11. The traditional stanza has grown into a monologue, not less lyrical than the refrain.

37 • THE MAIDEN'S COMPLAINT, page 144. *Pigens klage (Verden er fuld udaf falskhed og svig).* DgF 513G, see correction DgF X; Sch 152. * The poem, which in some versions is put into the mouth of a nun, is loosely built of stanzas some of which are found elsewhere. V. 2 is a type characteristically Continental: description of nature plus a more or less human analogy. Such a verse reminds about the flighty verse that in Southern Germany is called *Schnadahüpfeln.* Not less characteristic is the word *klafferne* (evil tongues) in v. 5. The vocable and the idea are alien to ballads, but common in later lyrical poetry, as a label for slanderers who make mischief.

II • HUMOR

7 • Jocular Songs

38 • THE WEDDING OF THE FLY, page 149. *Fluens bryllup (Den myg trækker op sine horn så blå).* GrN 14C, A-B quoted below as

No. 77. * The song is found in quite a few countries. This version deviates from other Scandinavian ones by the addition of verse 12–18 and is somewhat revised, probably by the publisher of the broadside. Ballad versions with meaningless choruses are not rare in the jocular song group. * 10 *fiddle:* in the original *lire,* an instrument (*drejelire,* hurdy-gurdy) that has now disappeared in Denmark.

39 . THE BANQUET OF THE BIRDS, page 151. *Fuglegildet (I skoven der holdtes et gilde så skøn).* ETK 13, according to Niels Madsen, Bratten. * This ditty is included to show the full background of the stunted *I skoven skulde være gilde* that is known by every Danish child. It is based on a common European tradition. * 29,1–2 [ ] means that these lines have been inserted from one of the other versions.

40 . THE MASTER'S COUNSEL, page 155. *Mesterens råd (En digt af ny jeg sjunge vil).* GrN 24, DaVi V, page 145, Sch 82 (under Spiritual Songs). * A sceptical and critical attitude towards women is a basic feature of the choice of subject matter in this group; neither are worries regarding choice of spouse a rare topic. This song is more surprising in its formulation and better composed than the majority.

41 . A BETTER BARGAIN, page 159. *Her bliver vel bedre køb (Ungersvend giljed han pigelil så).* GrN 27. * A typical humoristic tiff-dialogue, and quite clever: two inclining curves that meet in a surprising swoop, which is unusual for this group.

42 . THE LAD WHO WAS FOOLED, page 160. *Den narrede ungersvend (Skøn ridder og den lille mø).* ETK 52, according to Niels Mikkelsen. * Similar subjects in slight variations are often found in the ballads, see *e. g.* No. 34. Note the similarity and difference in the use of a related construction here and in the previous song. * 2 *joust,* in the Danish text *dyst,* Jutlandish for *shower;* here maybe *turn* or *round,* or a reminiscence of the ballad cliché *Den første dyst de sammen red:* When first they jousted . . .

43 . PEASANT'S WIFE VISITS COURTIER, page 162. *Bondens kone besøger hovmand (Bonden og hans hustru).* GrN 56C. * This jocular song, one of many of the same type, is not unlike ballads like No. 4 in regard to age, subject and expression; much of the amusement has probably from the very beginning been linked up with the tension between the ballad clichés and the ditty's general attitude. There is a

fixed intermediate refrain and a variable jocular refrain, a not unusual type (see DgF 390 *Lave og Jon,* which also has a long steady chorus).

44 • THE BIG CROW, page 164. *Den store krage (En bonde gik alt ved sin plov).* H. C. Frydendahl: *Fynske Folkeminder* I, 1945, according to Maren Jørgensen Bødkers; counterparts in GrN and ETK. * The song is common in Europe and this version is selected as an example of memory at its best: the informant's father was born c. 1787, she herself in 1841, and in 1942 H. C. Frydendahl managed to record 35 songs and fragments at her dictation. His publication seems to be the first Danish attempt to record a person's repertoire as a whole (see No. 59).

45 • UPSIDE DOWN DITTY, page 165. *Bagvendt vise (Ulven står på stalde).* GrN 91. * This still used type is known from all over Europe and degenerates often into nonsensical rigmaroles. The best stanzas are, of course, those that are easy to visualize. This version uses the concatenated stanza with one repeated line.

III • LATER SONGS

8 • Creed and Superstition

46 • THE TEN MAIDENS' SONG, page 169. *De ti jomfruers vise (Himmeriges rige lignes ved).* Sch 67; is mentioned, but not recorded before 1639. * The song is known in Denmark and Sweden, the chorus also in Norway. It is composed in the ballad form and atmosphere; only the last stanza moralizes, the rest is pure narrative (after Matthew 25). It continued to live in hymn books of the 17th century.

47 • JERUSALEM'S COBBLER, page 171. *Jerusalems skomager (O kristen sjæl og hjerte).* Sch 89. The only source, Niels Christensen's Song Book, ca. 1729, from which No. 28 is also taken, is from southeastern Jutland, see the Danish edition. The translator has felt free to use six or seven syllables in lines 1, 3, 6, and 7; the rest have six. The original has the characteristic hymn meter: 7676–6776 syllables. * A probably oriental legend about the man who behaved heartlessly towards the captured Christ, who answered him: "Thou shalt tarry till I come again," reached Europe in 1228, possibly transmitted by an Armenian archbishop. That the man was a Jewish cobbler named Ahasuerus, is

first related in a tendentious German popular book in 1602. It created quite an interest and it was printed in Denmark from 1607 onwards (see a full treatment in *Jahrbuch für Volksliedforschung* IX, 1964). It is very likely the source of the two Danish Ahasuerus songs; the later and more popular is presumably based on the otherwise unknown version printed here, which is older in style and tradition and also superior poetically. A pamphlet about Ahasuerus is mentioned in a lost edition from 1729; it is tempting to assume that this was nothing but a print of this version (confer v. 9,8: 1700 years) but the corruptions of our text are rather numerous, and its date, January 8, 1729 rather early for this assumption. * 11,5–8: Ahasuerus had, according to the tradition, hardly any money, as the Lord looked after him in his own way. This is the feature that is described here, but the original is nebulous. 12,8: *just like a smothered worm:* orig. *som dragens rede,* the meaning of which is doubtful. 13–15: the geographical names vary in the tradition, thus the translator has taken a certain freedom; *an Armenian around the river Kur* reflects the conjecture of the anthologist, as the *Kurperer* in the original cannot be definitely explained. There is no support to be found in the chapbook, but as mentioned the legend is possibly of Armenian origin. 16,7–8: the original sense is obscure but means, perhaps, that they were hardened in their ignorance and lack of understanding of the olden days (*i. e.* the passion of Christ, which they themselves had not witnessed). 18,5 and 8 do not rhyme; *Jews defying God:* orig. *Jøde vild* (wild Jew) makes room for any plausible guess. *Eghd: egenhændig:* with his own hands.

48 · THE MAID WHO TROD ON THE LOAF, page 176. *Pigen, der trådte på brødet (O menneske, jeg sjunge vil).* Sch 85. * This song, still sung in variations, has its roots in an old German song about events in Silbaco, Pomerania, but the motif is widely known. It is painted with broad and popular strokes and cannot, in its preserved form, be much older than the year 1800. As is well known, it inspired Hans Christian Andersen to write his fairy tale of the same name.

49 · THE RICH SISTER'S PUNISHMENT, page 180. *Rige søsters straf (Der var engang to søstre).* Sch 85. The composer Thorkild Knudsen has helpfully copied this song from his tape; the reporter is Johanne Bang from the island of Als, lying east of South Jutland. * This popular song, like No. 48, has an older German model. The poor rhymes are not caused by the translation into Danish – or English – as consistent rhyming, apparently, was not intended in the German song. Line 3 is repeated in singing, which allows for an occasional extra line.

50 • LIE AND TRUTH, page 182. *Løgn og Sandhed (I fordum tid var Sandhed mægtig og bold).* DaVi 9, see also DaVi V, p. 165, Sch 74; supplants another poem from the Danish edition. * The large group of later songs with historical and contemporary purpose rarely stands up to present-day reading. This and the following number, inserted here as samples, were first printed in 1547 on the same broadside and entitled: "Two beautiful Songs, one about Lie and Truth, the other about the Cassock." Both go back to the time before the triumph of the Reformation in 1536. *Lie and Truth* is the best of the religious war-song satires. Its evident objective was to adopt a European tradition of personifying Virtue and Sin, and from this point of view it is of less importance, whether or not the traditional opinion is right in pointing to Hans Tausen, the central figure among Denmark's church reformers, as the author. The song must, in any case, have been composed in 1533, when the early Protestantism suffered a setback and Tausen was banned from Sjælland by sentence of the bishop. This song is also in its place in an anthology of popular poetry by existing in several different recordings (with, among other things, a later conciliatory stanza) and in quite a few revised versions and translations.

51 • THE CASSOCK, page 185 (No. 52 in the Danish edition). *Munkekappen (O kappe, du est af Djævelen skabt).* DaVi 92, Sch 162. * This song attacking monastic orders is found in the same original print as the previous one. However, it is not Danish, but a free translation from the German, about 1530.

52 • MAY SONG, page 186 (No. 51 in the Danish edition). *En majvise (God dag, god dag, min ærlig' mand).* Sch 98–99, here after a modern recording with melody, printed earlier in *Folkesangen i Danmark,* edited by Thorkild Knudsen and Nils Schiørring after text in the Danish Folklore Archives, Vol. I, 1960. * Of all the religious and secular songs that were used at small and great festivities during the year, the May Song is the one that has kept alive the longest. Two song types are found: one secular, especially with roots in Jutland and East of Øresund, to which the one here reprinted belongs; and a religious type, composed by Peder Jensen Roskilde in the 1630's, supplanting the other, that was in the danger zone, because a royal ordinance of 1629 interfered with the use of secular songs. The inserted and final choruses of this category were: "Listen to our prayer, / Lord, be gracious and fair." Our song and the publication from which it is borrowed, prove that quite old song types can be found alive and in good condition even today. Compare No. 49.

9 • Romances

53 • THE TWO ROYAL CHILDREN, page 189. *De to kongebørn (Det var to ædelige kongebørn).* Sch 103, here according to *Det gamle Harboøre, Optegnelser af Karen Thuborg,* published by Henrik Ussing, 1928 (*Danmarks Folkeminder* 36). * The myth about Hero and Leander in Ovid's version has been highly popular in European folk poetry and has been linked together with other motifs. The Danish ballad is based upon one of the many German song types dealing with the same subject *(Die Königskinder);* in Denmark alone more than thirty recordings of the music are known apart from records of the text without music made in the course of the last 300 years.

54 • DANYSER ("Tannhäuser"), page 191. *(Velan, jeg her begynde vil).* DaVi 60, Sch 108. * The ballad is translated from Low German, its melody is found in Hans Thomissøn's Hymnbook of 1569, the most important Danish hymnal published in the century of the Reformation. The Austro-Bavarian troubadour Tannhäuser (13th century) was linked up with numerous legends and tales, *i. a.* an Italian story (perhaps originally a Celtic legend) about life in the mountain of erotic love (of course regarded as a deadly sin by the Church) and a legend about the arid staff that burst into leaf (and thus a criticism of the Pope's rejection of the truly repentant). The contradiction between these two trends leads to varying conclusions in the original versions, right up to the redemption motif of Richard Wagner's opera. * 1 typical introductory formula, compare No. 55. 17,2: the German ballad reads: "with (her) good will and safe-conduct". 18: Urban IV was Pope 1261–64, the historic Tannhäuser lived 1200–68. 30–31 seem to have been added by the Danish translator.

55 • COBBLER AND NOBLEMAN, page 195. *Skomager og edelmand (Hører til, I herrer store og små).* DaVi 62, Sch 109. * This erotic short story, that might have belonged in the Decameron, treats a broadly popular subject in a rare double form and formally it is typical of the narrative song of the time. The prelude "O harken, my lords"; the moralizing end, which, however, can hardly be taken seriously; the smoothly progressing story which is not only undecorated but also unstylized and almost without tension, does not belong to a ballad but to a *roman;* although in size and in the number of events it corresponds to the ballad of chivalry. Verse 31 tells us that it is a translation; an independent version is found in Swedish, but the sup-

posed German model has never been found. ⁎ 19–20: in inverse order in the Danish version. 21,3 and 24 are obscure. 31,1: "He who translated this song into Danish."

10 · Stories about Love

56 · THE LOST FALCON, page 201. *Den bortfløjne falk (Jeg red mig ud spadsere).* DaVi 82, Sch 139. ⁎ An emotional story with little action, about a jilted maiden who, despite her loss, lets herself be consoled. The falcon is, of course, an image. Vedel has edited the text thoroughly, possibly based on another source than that of the scribe. Some of his emendations have been inserted here without comments. According to Vedel, a verse is missing between 7 and 8, beginning with "The maiden pledged the lord her troth/ let . . ."

57 · WATCHMAN'S SONG, page 203. *En vægtervise (Den vinters nat gøres kold og lang).* DaVi 65, Sch 115. ⁎ An interesting group among the predominantly epic songs is formed by the Watchmen's Songs, which as regards circumstances and environment are genuinely courteous and medieval, and which correspond to the German *Tagelied* and the Franco-Provençal *Alba.* The famous *Heart Book* (the oldest Danish song book, written 1553–55 and cut out in heart form) opens with this popular sample of the group (there not too well edited) and includes several others. The watchman is the confidant of loving couples – Brangäne's rôle in the second act of Wagner's *Tristan and Isolde.* ⁎ 1 *around the castle:* original *forborgen* (secret) possibly a mistake of *foran borgen:* outside the castle. The translation of the next line is free. 6 *virtue* (of love): chivalrous tradition and Lutheran morality – and also because wooing at night was a custom of the time. 8,7–8 are reversed.

58 · THE THREE NOBLEMEN, page 205. *De tre grever (Skøn jomfru hun stander på det højeste bjerg).* Sch 132, here from the same source as No. 53. ⁎ The oldest version of this song appeared in 15th century Germany. It was extremely popular both there and in Scandinavia. The ending varies; the Harboöre version is sad and keeps to the clichés of the late ballad, with the insertion of the bayonet as an amusing innovation; other versions have happy endings. Fragments have been used in children's song plays that often preserve very old relics of "grownup" forms of poetry.

59 · THE RE-UNION, page 207. *Genkendelsen (En stjerneklar aften i Roligheds Lund).* Sch 121, according to *Selma Nielsens Viser,* published by Nils Schiørring, 1956 (*Danmarks Folkeminder* 66); this publication is important, as it prints 100 songs with melodies from the repertoire of a single person. * A theme frequently used has here – hardly before c. 1800 – found a particularly felicitous form, felicitous in the sense that the song contains all the ingredients that make for the greatest popularity. It is thus typical of the newer stratum of *skillingsvise* (penny-song) or *flyveblad* (broadside), the colossal industry that began to decline about 1900 without having as yet fully disappeared. The translator has changed the names to suit; the original *(Hertug) Karl, Ludvig* and *Lise* were names in vogue around 1800.

11. The Woman Worshipped

60 · PER RÆV LILLE'S LOVE SONG, page 210. *Per Ræv Lilles kærlighedsvise (Ret elskovens dyd med sang og fryd).* DaVi 290B, Sch 12, here according to *En Klosterbog fra Middelalderens Slutning* (A Convent Book From the Closing of the Middle Ages), *AM 76, 8°,* published by Marius Kristensen, 1933. * This poem heads a manuscript of theological miscellanies with quite a few Marian poems. Several of these are by the otherwise unknown Per Ræv Lille ("Peter Fox Little") to whom this song may possibly be attributed. But variants of stanzas 1, 2, and 5 are found in the Heart Book (1553–55), see notes to No. 57. Its appearance in *Klosterbogen* has for decades prompted a debate among scholars as to whether the song is to be ranged alongside the Convent Book's other erotically tinted troubadour poems which undoubtedly are dedicated to the Holy Virgin (thus, Hans Brix, H. Grüner-Nielsen, Oluf Friis); or, whether as the only one of its type, it must be considered a secular courteous poem of love, despite its inclusion in the book which in that case must have been caused by the Christian expressions it contains (thus, Brandt & Helveg, Erland Hjärne, Ernst Frandsen, F. J. Billeskov Jansen, also Nils Schiørring and Helge Toldberg). That the anthologist of the *Heart Book* represents the latter idea does not signify much. He could hardly have had much affinity with the mystical currents of the later Middle Ages. – Supporting the "worldly school", we include this poem as the most intense exponent of our chapter title and as the earliest and most complete song relevant to this anthology to come down to us. Marian poetry and courteous poetry have furnished Per Ræv Lille with his rich splendor in words

and images which to some degree is related to that of the following songs but which in these is toned down. * 1,1 is also found in No. 57, 6,3; this may be incidental, but both songs appear in the *Heart Book.* 1,3 *won't pronounce:* in the original *ej nævne vil; ej* is omitted in the *Heart Book,* but Grüner-Nielsen must be wrong in regarding this as authentic. 2,2, 2,4 and 5,12 are echoes from *The Elf Hill,* our No. 3. 2,3 *know . . . woe:* this rhyme scheme was intended for the first and third line of all stanzas, but was not carried through in the original. 4, 3–4: love was never more sublimely unselfish!

61 • HIS SWEETHEART'S DEATH, page 212. *Den kærestes død (Den stund der verden hun ginges mig med).* DaVi 159, Sch 149. * The chorus that is usually fixed in its wording, has here two forms, corresponding to the change in the song. It is a poetical effect, not a functional dance chorus as in the ballad. * 2 *mien and manner:* in the original *lader og lemper* (behavior), a set phrase.

62 • A SAD COMPLAINT OF SEPARATION, page 213. *Et bedrøveligt klagemål over skilsmisse (Skilsmis, ak skilsmis, hvi est du så hård).* Sch 146. The broadside reprinted here is the oldest version. * This love lament has much of later poetical phrasing, even foreign words (5,1 *firmament,* and others in the original), but preserved the fine but rare "Proud-Eline"-ballad-stanza, named thus after DgF 210, with the abbreviated 2nd and 4th lines, to which is added a full varied chorus. An artistic and moving poem. * 18 *Tobias:* the name of a popular biblical apocryph, which was dealt with in *Tobiae Komedie,* about 1600 (by H. Justesen Ranch?).

63 • THE BEAUTIFUL TREE, page 217. *Det fagre træ (Jeg ved ihvor et træ det stander).* DaVi 271, Sch 146. Here, as in several other ballads and songs, the nature symbol for woman is a tree, see also No. 5; the song, however, is known only in this version. It is possible that it should have been written in ten quatrains. * 4 *slanderer,* in the original *klaffer,* a stock character in the genre, see No. 37.

64 • A HEART SO TRUE, page 219. *(Et trofast hjerte af al min agt).* DaVi 250, Sch 146. * This song is typical of the rather abstract and stiff, but naïve and often intense, love poetry of the period. It has possibly had an additional stanza, se No. 79. * 2 *traducer: klaffer,* see No. 63. 2,6 *way:* in original *ry, rej:* dance, behavior.

65 • ROSINA, page 220. *(Rosina, hvor varst du så bold).* DaVi 286, Sch 147. * This song, translated from the German, seems to have been written by a very young man; it smells of paper and ink, which precisely is its charm. The Paris verse may pass, but the allusions to Vergil's Aeneid, to the novel *Pontus and Sidonia* and to Chrestien de Troyes' novel about Ywain the Lion Knight and Miss Luneta, are too much for this slender frame. The Pontus verse is found in German and in a differing version in the same manuscript, but not in our text, whose last stanza is found only here.

66 • HAPPINESS IN LOVE, page 221. *Kærlighedslykke (Urterne gror, og solen hun skin).* DaVi 209, Sch 151. * The relationship between stanza 1 and 2 corresponds to the relationship between stanza 1 and 2 of No. 37, *q. v.* The song is loosely constructed of sententious stanzas *("stev")* and is found in several Danish and Swedish versions with the cards shuffled.

67 • ERIK LANGE TO SOPHIE BRAHE, page 222. *E. L. til S. B. (Lad fare, min sjæl, din høje attrå).* DaVi 213, Sch 144. * This poem holds the top position in the love poetry of the 16th century due to its pithiness and intensity, its ingenious parallels and contradictions, and its peculiar imagery. It asserts its position without further explanation in spite of a few blemishes in transmission. It has created special interest since the analysis by means of which Hans Brix (*Analyser og Problemer,* IV, 1938) establishes an author and an addressee, and connects the poem with another that, though of less grandeur, holds a similarly high position among the poems of the period written by or ascribed to women. Although the time of the handing-down of the poem makes this combination doubtful, we have, nevertheless, put the two poems together as No. 67 and No. 68, under titles that correspond to Brix's theory. Here it suffices to report that the well-to-do squire Erik Lange fell in love with Tycho Brahe's beautiful and learned sister Sophie (probably during her first marriage, if the poem is really his). After having been a widow for two years in 1590 she became engaged to Erik Lange, who was then already heavily in debt because of alchemy and other nebulous ventures; but they were not married until 1602, a couple of years after she had gone to see him during his wanderings; he died in 1613, she in 1643. – Like his teacher, Tycho Brahe, and this great astronomer's sister, Lange was conversant with the world of ideas on which stanzas like 3, 8, and 13 are based; and although, as mentioned before, the appearance of the poem in a manu-

script from 1584 is a little difficult to explain, it must be remembered that this manuscript goes back to Queen Sophie who had connections with Tycho Brahe's circle and his astronomical and astrological research center on the island of Hven in the Øresund. (It was at a meeting there with Anders Sørensen Vedel that the Queen offered suggestions which resulted in his collection of ballads in 1591). – During their long engagement Sophie Brahe wrote a Latin poem to Erik Lange (or, at least, a draft of it), also in nature-mystical terminology. There is a long distance from this to No. 68, which is supposed to date from the same period and to have been written for an otherwise unknown occasion (see notes to No. 68, v. 28). The possibility cannot be excluded that Erik Lange, during his economic and social eclipse, did receive internal and external promptings to seek a rich marriage. Sophie Brahe's poem – if she really were the author – is somewhat broad and formally not on the same level as his; but while much of the love poetry of that time was enmeshed in lightly melancholic abstraction, in this poem the real love, the pride and the uncertainty of a genuine human being is speaking. ⁕ 1 *destiny:* in the original *forsæt,* which means both the human plans and the ruling force of destiny. 3 imagery from the Phoenix myth. From here on the poet turns against the despair of the first stanzas, and a long series of contrasting similarities between 1, 3, and 4 etc. can be observed, see No. 68. v. 50. 6 see No. 37. 8 superstition about guardian spirits. 11,2 reconstructed after erasure. 11,3 better in other versions. 15,1–3 see No. 64.

12 • The Woman Longing

68 • SOPHIE BRAHE TO ERIK LANGE, page 225. *S. B. til E. L. (Nu vil jeg for eder kvæde).* DaVi 166, Sch 149. ⁕ See notes to No. 67. ⁕ 1–2 standard introductory formula; not until v. 3 is the addressee mentioned directly. 7 criticism of the text is difficult, and we use Brix's conjectures. 12,4 *would celebrate:* in the original "to a feast" or "to a party", is meant ironically. 16,1 orig. *trommeter, symfoni og strengespil:* drums, hurdy-gurdy and strings. 28,4 orig. "among bog-myrtles *(pors)* in . . ." *Pors* is also a family name, and the Pors family lived in the same part of the country as the Lange family – perhaps an allusion to the name? 30,1 *(longing) is . . .* thus in the original, but corrected in DaVi to *oc* meaning *and* (see No. 64, v. 1,7). 34 *at my own table:* in other words, she is either married or a widow with her own home. 50,4 like No. 67, v. 5, but passive.

69 · THE NIGHTINGALE SENT TO THE KING, page 232. *Nattergal sendes til kongen (Far vel, du ædle nattergal).* DaVi 191. ∗ Although the motif of a bird sent as messenger is anything but original, this song belongs to the very best of its time, with loftiness and submission combined. No parallels are known. ∗ 1 *crimson:* in the original *rød;* version B, which deviates in many points and is of small value, has *lystige:* merry. 5,4 freely translated.

70 · DISAPPOINTMENT OVERCOME, page 235. *Overvunden skuffelse (En ungersvend, var mådelig skøn).* DaVi 142. ∗ This song is not clear in all details and an existing B text is preserved in an even worse form. It is nevertheless included as a sample of a hardier mood than usual, especially in poems ascribed to women. ∗ 3,5–7 partly borrowed from B. 5,3 in the original the whole line appears in Low German: *rop nicht so ludigen: gewunden spyll* (do not shout so loudly: the game is won), possibly sloppiness in the translation or for effect.

71 · 'TWAS ON A SATURDAY EVENING, page 236. *Det var en lørdag aften.* Sch 150; according to Fr. Sneedorff-Birch: *Danske Folkeviser og Melodier. 1. Pentade,* 1837. ∗ The fine, broad version now commonly known was written by Svend Grundtvig, based on a popular song. We reproduce this in its earliest printed form. The song is popular all over Denmark and Sweden, often in better and longer versions. A note to the one used here says: "From the Aarhus region (Zeuthen)."

72 · THE JILTED MAID, page 237. *Den forskudte pige (Jeg går i tusind tanker).* A. P. Berggreen's *Danske Folkesange og Melodier,* 3rd edition, 1869, No. 117. ∗ Deviating from the Danish edition of this book, we are using the original MSS of Berggreen's collection in the Danish Folklore Archives. The tune has been recorded in the Frederiksborg area. Its four verses are the essence of a longwinded broadside song with an attempt at action, printed in Julius Strandberg's popular collection *Den syngende Mand paa Bølge og Land.* The transformation from the lyric to the epic is a characteristic process.

73 · THE ROSE OF LOVE, page 238. *Kærlighedsrosen (En yndig og frydefuld sommertid).* Sch 147, same source as No. 72 (No. 106). ∗ Berggreen used the title "The Maid sings", but as is the case with many similar songs, this one is sometimes put into the mouth of a man and sometimes into that of a woman. It is perhaps the finest and most popular of the lyrical love songs. The old symbol of the rose unfolds

itself spontaneously from the text. The comments of Berggreen's correspondent are not printed in our Danish edition, and the better choice of the source for Nos. 72–73 is due to the advice of Thorkild Knudsen.

IV • ADDENDUM

13 • Addendum

74 • MEDIEVAL FRAGMENTS, page 243. Although the ballad in its origin is a genre of the Middle Ages (in spite of the fact that a certain number of them are composed after the end of this period), and though the poetry of the aristocratic song books must be based on a partly medieval tradition, only negligible fragments have been preserved from the Middle Ages. Most of these have been printed literally in this chapter and have been translated in the notes. With the exception of *d,* all of them are pen tests written in accidental empty places in very different manuscripts.

a: The Cologne Verse, pen test in a manuscript from Cologne, probably from before 1250: "I know a lady in the world to be,/ her (life) I honor ardently". This rhyme falls well in line with the German lyrical tradition, which later on manifested itself copiously; *her life* see No. 60.

b: The Skåning Verse, about 1300 in AM 37,4°: "The honest Scanians, you must agree,/ have never swallowed an injury". It is not known from which context this rhyme was taken.

c: The Rune Verse, about 1300, insertion in Codex Runicus from the Scanian Law, AM 28,8°: "Dreamt myself a dream last night/ 'bout silk and beautiful furs." The melody written for these lines (from which is taken the identification signal of Denmark's Radio, program I) continues without text for a space that corresponds to two text lines; but there is no room for the music for a possible chorus. It is, however, probable that we are here in the world of the ballad.

d: The Greenland Verse, DgF 19D (vol. X). "A man abides at a Greenland stream,/ the name Spieldebeth he had;/ and he has more of silver white/ than others of pork so fat./ *From the North it comes in again o'er the sand.*" – No other verse has been preserved in such a peculiar way as this. About 1425 the cartographer Claudius Clavus from the island of Funen drew a map of Scandinavia including Greenland. The map became of great geographical-historical importance, and it is possible that Clavus himself visited Greenland. When he lacked names for rivers and promontories, he named them according to rigmaroles, and on the Greenland map he used names as DER cape, BOR river, EN cape, MAND river etc. Thus one can read a whole verse: "*Der bor en mand . . .*" (there lives a man) with a defective chorus, strongly colored by the dialect of West Funen (*eynh* = *en:* one; *heyde* = *hedde:* is named; *feyde* = *fede:* fat; *hanyd* = *han:* he, expressing the *j*-colored *n*). The verse was originally regarded as an unusual lampoon (*nidefildh* = *feld med nider:* fur with lice). Later on a connection with a verse in a Swedish form of No. 21 was pointed out; this led to the assumption that *nidefildh* is a distortion in the writing of *uidesølf* (white silver) and *hanh* in line 4 of *andre* (others). In this case the verse is a regular Funen version of DgF 19, of Swedish origin, and without mockery or humor. The chorus is defective. It has been interpreted as "The North wind drifts the sand again" or "From the North (it) drifts (in on the) sand now, now." The relationship with the chorus of No. 21 is in any case obvious.

e: The Marsk Stig Chorus, pertinent to DgF 145G, our No. 14, inserted in several empty spaces in a theological manuscript NkS 123,4°, Ribe ca. 1460 (DgF X). There is nothing new in the text, but it is good to find a basic part of our greatest poetical cycle of the Middle Ages preserved in such an old source.

f: Lyric Prelude, pen test ca. 1520 in a mixed Swedish-Latin-Danish manuscript AM 792,4°: "Just lately I took part in a dance,/ I saw two roses beside me stand." Quite typical in the lyrical style. (*f, g, h* were first printed, together with other small discoveries, in *Danske Studier,* 1918).

g: Parody-Rhyme, on a blank page of a theological manuscript, AM 783,4°, from the 15th century: "I have dreamt a dream last night,/ it was of a cat/ and also of a dog/ and of a troll." The dream gives the impression of a parody on a verse of the rune-type.

h: Humoristic Lines, pen test from about 1500 in a Swedish legal manuscript AM 46,4°: "Please, dear mother, you make me some mush,/ my maidenhead's showed far up in my crotch." Parallels are not known; this is possibly a fragment of a jocular song. Other pen tests from the same source are Marian poetry.

i: Aase and Karonelle, on the parchment cover of the Upsala University Library, MS C 65,4°, possibly from 1500–20: "Madam Aase and Madam Karonelle they practiced ... the dance." The defective lines have been printed before, though in a bad reading, in the postscript to *Svenska Fornskrift-Sällskapets Samlingar* XXIV, 3, G. Klemming's edition of *Svenska Medeltids-Postillor,* and their reading cannot be made complete. Nothing is certain as regards the meaning of these words, but they deserve to be known because it is most probable that they formed the prelude to a song in the light genre.

k: The Knight in Deerskin • Ridder i hjorteham (Det var herre Peder). DgF 67A, inserted in a Swedish-Norwegian theological manuscript from about 1450, Linköping. The ballad is only a fragment of a late ballad dealing with metamorphosis (Sir Peder gains access to the maiden by transforming himself). The Linköping manuscript contains the only ballad that was written down in a regular manner during the Middle Ages. It is furthermore of interest because it begins with the chorus which is still sung today as prelude to a song-dance on the Faroe islands, serving as a kind of an introduction to the melody. In the manuscript it is placed a little above the first verse, like a title.

I've dreamt about sweet maidens, night after night.

It happened that Sir Peder
spoke to his squires two:
"Could you get me proud Aase-lille
by winsome talk by you?"
I've dreamt about the maiden, night after night.

Away then went the mail-clad squires
to where proud Aase-lille stayed:
"My lord he is aboard his ship,
he wants to see you, proud maid."

Answered them proud Aase-lille,
she answered them with a word:
"It is not the way of a maid
to say yes and go aboard.

It is not the way of a maid
to say yes and go aboard;
shame and disgrace will follow her home
and many a scathing word."

Back they went, the mail-clad squires
and told their master and lord:
"Proud Aase-lille we could not get
with many a winsome word."

"You couldn't get proud Aase-lille
with many a winsome word;
I'll hex me into a deerskin,
then surely I will get her."

One of his skins was of silver white,
the other of gold so red;
and it was Sir Peder
so joyfully he played.

75 • LAVE STISEN AND LADY ELINE, page 245. *Lave Stisøn og fru Eline (Det var skøn Ellensborg).* DgF 259H, compare with the shorter version No. 27. ⁂ The varying length of the many recordings of this ballad is not caused by the usual dilution, but by a peculiar shifting of the plot. The many versions belong to the period of the aristocratic song books (the exact time of their recording seems to be of no importance), but they can be arranged according to a highly interesting development as Grundtvig has done. B (19 verses) is not very different from A, but is softened *inter alia* by a dialogue between the three parties, after Lave has maltreated his wife. C (31 v.) extends the B plot, and at the end Espen kicks in the door and kills Lave. D (27 v.) adds another feature: Ellensburg does not die from the maltreatment, but is cast off to become a servant as Lave wants to marry his mistress who had told him about the other two. Nevertheless, he takes pity on her in a beautiful dialogue (like v. 45–47). E (59 v.) does not, in spite of its length, give much space to the story of A–C, and the main interest lies in the description of the wedding, Ellensburg's humiliation, and the conciliation; furthermore, Lave's mother starts playing the rôle of the victim's defender. F has the typical verbosity of Karen Brahe's renowned folio-manuscript (69 v.) and represents a free version with new features. G and H (46 and 59 verses) are based on

the E-type: as in E, Ellensburg is humiliated, locked up, and disowned, but the corporal maltreatment, whose fatal consequence had disappeared long ago, is absent. G is still bound to the older phases of development, while H contains omissions, deviations, and new features. Some of them, despite their novelty, may be traced back to the ballad about the patient woman which from the D-stage and onwards is combined with the Lave ballad. Lastly, I presents a deliberately rewritten version, while H, according to Grundtvig's expression, still belongs to the "*folk-poetical* development or degeneration of our ballad". – This sketchy outline gives an idea of the evolutionary possibilities of the ballad by change of time, place and taste, and of the intricacy of research. The one who, without preparation, reads the first and the last stages, A and H, in this book, will find similarities in only a few episodes at the beginning, which in A and H, nevertheless, are so different in importance and with such dissimilar solutions, that A and H in their tone and plot look like two entirely different poems. The demonstrations of their connection is one of Grundtvig's most brilliant and profitable individual studies. Only in rare cases is the material so pedagogically clear, being without newer traditions or foreign versions but copious within its own limits. – We have used a few minor changes from DgF.

76 • THE DICE GAME, page 254. *Terningspillet (Jeg vil ha' den jomfru).* DgF 238R (vol. X), according to Jensine Hansen of Ulfborg Lake, Madum district. Compare the full version No. 33. * The great scholarly editions must display all the material. A book like ours can only bring a little of the best. This specimen of E. T. Kristensen's thousands of diary pages has been inserted to show how unimportant and uncertain the reports may be that the researcher has to fit into the whole. In this particular case the recording is of no value as the song was widely known beforehand, even in the informant's own district; but it is important to point out that even such insignificant fragments as these may be of the greatest value; they could, for instance, be the sole proof of the existence in a given area of song types known in other places.

77 • THE WEDDING OF THE FLY, page 254. *Fluens bryllup (Bremsens bud kom ridend i Gaard).* GrN 14AB; Hans Mikkelsen Ravn (Corvinus): *Ex Rhythmologia Danica Epitome Brevissima,* Sorö 1649, here in translation after *Danske Metrikere* I, 1953, edited by Arthur Arnholtz, Erik Dal and Aage Kabell. * In his book Ravn

gives rules for the theories of metrics and language of the late Renaissance. Nevertheless, he preserved an ear for the old folk poetry and gives *inter alia* a fine analysis of the ballad metres and choruses. We shall only print one of the examples consisting of two variants of the Fly Song. Their choruses (parodical Latinate words in C) are both found again in recent Scandinavian records. Ravn concludes with a masterly characterization of the chorus. In another of his books he gives advice regarding the recording of folk tunes, based on oral report.

78 · FAITHLESSNESS, page 255. *Verdens troløshed (Her er ingen tro på jorden).* DaVi 131. ∗ Lyrical songs with themes other than love are exceptions; their subject-matter is suggested by this pessimistic poem which is only included in the appendix because it is alien to the other chapters of this book. It cannot be denied that a strong element of tradition or sheer convention is part of this piece – as in so many of the love songs – the mood of which, however, must be considered to be typical of its period. ∗ 4,7–8 the sensitiveness seems to border almost on irritation but this impression is hardly correct.

79 · O LORD, O LORD, A HEART SO TRUE, page 256. *Et trofast hjerte, o Herre min.* Hans Christensen Sthen's *Vandrebog,* from about 1609, here according to the commentary of DaVi 250, Sch 35. ∗ In the history of hymns the re-fashioning of a Catholic hymn into a Lutheran, of a secular song into a hymn, the use of a profane melody for a godly song, etc., is generally known. In this hymn by Sthen the italicized words have their parallels in the original song as we know it. Let us add that another version of No. 64 reverses verses 3 and 4, as Sthen does. Possibly he had known the song in a version with five stanzas. By the insertion of *you* in 5,3–4, the result is, in any case, a perfect song fragment, and in the rest of it only *Jesus Our Lord* along with most of 5,7 need to be Sthen's. His hymn was current during the 17th and 18th centuries and has been revived in the Danish hymn books of the present century.

15 · INDICES

STANDARD EDITIONS AND OTHER LITERATURE

The four main sources of the present anthology

DgF = *Danmarks gamle Folkeviser,* 1853 ff. I–IX: Text edition by Svend Grundtvig, Axel Olrik, H. Grüner-Nielsen. X: Text addenda by H. Grüner-Nielsen, Karl-Ivar Hildeman, Erik Dal, Iørn Piø, completed 1965. Vols. I–X have been reprinted with new prefaces in English, Copenhagen, 1966–67. XI: Melody edition by H. Grüner-Nielsen, Nils Schiørring, Thorkild Knudsen (in progress). XII: Index volume (in preparation).

ETK = *Et hundrede gamle danske skjæmteviser efter nutidssang, samlede og for størstedelen optegnede af Evald Tang Kristensen.* Århus, 1901.

GrN = *Danske Skæmteviser (Folkeviser og litterær Efterklang) efter Visehaandskrifter fra 16.–18. Aarh. og Flyveblade, udg. af H. Grüner-Nielsen.* Copenhagen, 1927–28. Still available.

DaVi = *Danske Viser fra Adelsvisebøger og Flyveblade 1530–1630, udg. af H. Grüner-Nielsen.* I–VII, Copenhagen, 1912–31.

Other works with many references concerning single ballads

Sch = Niels Schiørring: *Det 16. og 17. århundredes verdslige danske visesang,* I–II. Dissertation, Copenhagen 1950. References in the present volume indicate page numbers in Vol. I.

Erik Dal: *Nordisk folkeviseforskning siden 1800. Omrids af text- og melodistudiets historie og problemer især i Danmark.* Copenhagen, 1956. Summary: Scandinavian ballad research, pp. 410–430, continued in *Scandinavica* I, 1962. Still available.

Axel Olrik: *Danske Folkeviser i Udvalg.* I–II, Copenhagen, 1899–1909. Vol. I is the classical anthology for school use and includes a fine general introduction. Superseded by Ernst Frandsen: *Danske Folkeviser i Udvalg,* 1937, and later.

See also the large histories of Danish literature, *e. g.* Carl S. Petersen, Oluf Friis, Gustav Albeck *et al.,* and *Nordisk Kultur,* Vols. 9, 24, 25, 1931–34.

Annotated melody editions

A. P. Berggreen: *Danske Folkesange og Melodier,* 3. udg. Copenhagen, 1869. With piano settings.

Gamle danske Viser, udg. af Arthur Arnholtz og Nils Schiørring under Medvirken af Finn Viderø. I–V, Copenhagen 1939 and later. Still available. With piano settings.

Folkevisen i Danmark, redigeret af Thorkild Knudsen and Nils Schiørring efter optegnelser i Dansk Folkemindesamling. Instalments 1960 ff., still available.

LIST OF SOURCES

This list is a mere repetition of the references given at the song titles of this book. Further information is available in the source editions, especially in the chapter about the manuscripts in DaVi VI. The real purpose of the list is to demonstrate that a systematic enumeration of the relevant sources also becomes almost chronological. The manuscript sources group themselves clearly: the mss. of the nobility, the few peasants' songbooks, and, much later, the recordings from the 19. and 20. centuries (melodies dating back to about 1810). The broadsides were published uninterruptedly during the centuries, while Vedel/Syv's editions appeared 1591–1787. In addition, a few ballads and songs are found in scattered written and printed sources with other purposes.

Medieval sources

Various manuscripts about 1200–1550 (pen tests): 74 *a–k*
Theological miscellany ("Klosterbog") about 1470–80: 60

Songbooks of the nobility

The Heart Book 1553–55: 57 64
Jens Bille's Ms. 1555–59: 66
Langebek's Quarto Ms. 1562–80: 45 61 63 65 69
Svaning's Ms. I c. 1580: 5 24 36 56 70
Svaning's Ms. II c. 1580: 8 12 15 16
Valentin Rentzel's Ms. 1580–90: 13 14
Karen Brahe's Folio Ms. c. 1583: 4 23 29
Queen Sophia's Ms. 1584: 34 67
Anna Urop's Ms. c. 1610: 78
Anna Basse's Ms., before 1616: 18 21 35
Sofia Sandberg's Ms., before 1622: 25

Ida Giøe's Ms. c. 1630: 11 43 55 68
Langebek's Folio Ms. c. 1630: 20 22 75
The Smaller Stockholm Ms. 1641: 26
Vibeke Bild's Greater Folio Ms. 1646 ff.: 40 41

Peasants' songbooks
Songbook from Als, South Jutland, c. 1700: 33
Niels Christensen's Songbook, Southwest Jutland, c. 1729: 28 **47**

Other old manuscripts
Anders Sivenssøn's report to Ole Worm, Scania 1624: 27

Broadsides
1547: 52 1580: 54 1610: 50 1648: 62
shortly before 1800: 37 38 48

Other old prints
Anders Sørensen Vedel's Ballad Book, 1591: 17
(Hans Christensøn Sthen's Vandrebog, c. 1600: 79)
Joachim Moltke: Aandelig Haandbog, 1639: 46
Hans Mikkelsen Ravn (Corvinus): Rhythmologia Danica, 1649: **77**
Peder Syv's augmented edition of Vedel's Ballad Book, 1695: 2
Erik Pontoppidan: Everriculum fermenti veteris, 1736: 9

Recordings from popular tradition, included in editions 1837 ff.
Around Aarhus, East Jutland, Zeuthen 1837: 71
. . . C. Schütz 1843: 73
South Zealand, Franziska Carlsen 1844–46: 10 31
Zealand, H. V. Fiedler 1847: 7
North Zealand, A. P. Berggreen c. 1850: 72
Thy, Northwest Jutland, A. C. Povlsen-Dal 1855: 30
West Jutland, Evald Tang Kristensen 1868–95: 6 76
Jutland, the same: 39 42
Lemvig, Northwest Jutland, Peder Kr. Madsen 1870: 32
West Jutland, P. K. Toksvig 1870: 1
Glostrup near Copenhagen, J. N. Vinther c. 1876: 19
Harboøre, Northwest Jutland, Karen Thuborg: 53 58
Zealand, Selma Nielsen: 59
Funen, H. C. Frydendahl 1942: 44
Himmerland, East Jutland, Thorkild Knudsen's tapes 1959–61: **49 51**

TITLES, • FIRST LINES, AND *DANISH TITLES*

In one alphabet, with references to numbers. The italicized *Danish titles* include a few first lines but exclude certain titles beginning with names. The articles are included in the titles, but *The, Den, Det, De* are disregarded when alphabetizing.